gracing

gracing

HANNAH PACKARD CROWTHER

FaithMatters

FM

Faith Matters Publishing
2929 W Navigator Drive, Suite 400
Meridian, ID 83642
faithmatters.org

Editing support from Jana Riess.

Out Of A Stone by Thomas Keating copyright © 2018
A Rising Tide of Silence LLC

To request permissions,
contact the publisher at info@faithmatters.org.

Printed in the United States of America

ISBN: 978-1-953677-20-4 (paperback) |
978-1-953677-21-1 (ebook) | 978-1-953677-22-8 (audiobook)

Library of Congress Number: 2024939939

10 9 8 7 6 5 4 3 2 1

To Miriam—
    One of the Gatherers,
    Wayfinders,
    and Wholemakers

CONTENTS

Grace as a noun transforms into *gracing*—a verb.
The phenomenon is participatory,
Collaborative.
Something like flow.
A partnership of anchored flight,
Shells gathered from a generous shore.
It's living in heaven while standing on earth

—Like being joined at the hip with GOD.

A Parable of Grace

Once I was a bird.

Newly hatched, I peeked cautiously beyond the edge of my nest. The world was so much larger and grander on this side of the shell. Wisps of white hung tenuously in blue above, and the green of vibrant earth invited from below. Like a siren's call, the world sang out.

I stretched my wings wide, breathing deep the sunny warmth. But when I stepped forward impetuously, a clump of crusted mud and shell broke loose from the edge of my nest. It tumbled down through twigs and branches, and landed, shattering on the ground.

Alarmed, I retreated to the safety of my feather bed. I pulled myself close and deep.

And I waited.

The stillness broke just moments later when a rush of birds spilled suddenly from a neighboring tree. Fearful for their fate, I called loudly—an open-mouthed squawk to warn of dangerous collisions with the ground.

But to my surprise, the birds went up into the blue instead of down into the green. Their elegant bodies ascended as if by transparent threads—their wings unchained. I was disarmed.

I again stretched my wings—tentatively but with new hope. Against all reason, I leapt blindly from the safety of my nest. Fighting desperately against the pull, I flapped wildly, unsure as to which direction I was headed . . . until I heard the thud.

Opening my eyes, I saw the broken fragments of shell by my side. My painful rump told all. Above me, I heard the birds calling, leaping again from the safety of their tree and sweeping the sky in a massive undulating pool—unbounded.

Again I cried to these paradoxes of nature, these beauties untethered by the force that held me down. Why couldn't I join them? Why couldn't I understand? Where was help?

As if in response, a cool breath touched my wings. Time slowed and my feathers hovered—barely reaching for the birds above.

And then in a moment, I understood.

The empty space between me and the blue was not empty at all. It was saturated with something of heft as real as me. It permeated all the holes. It was the paint between all the sticks and leaves and mountains and birds within my view.

It was simple, really—just air.

But also, it was everything.

Transformed, I again spread my wings wide. My efforts were no longer a fight. No digging deep. Like light dissipating darkness, a morning thought dissipating a dream, clarity dissipated my unknowing—my reaching.

Running forward now, all at once my feet broke free of the ground. I tucked them close behind me. And I flapped my wings not despite absence, but in response to presence. Like a mother with palms cupped and lowered, the air lifted me. Gathered me. Delivered me whole to the blue.

Now finally windborne, I sailed, dancing through unbridled sky—all my prior struggles understood for this moment. Finally joining the others, I was saved—the measure of my creation now full.

Gracing, I flew.

Collecting

When I was a girl, I loved wandering the shore to find works of art, like gifts, in the sand. Creamy pink shells that curled into themselves; ordinary grayish-white clam shells, hinged precariously to their other halves; and iridescent mirrors guarded in hairy mussel shells. Even now that I'm a grown woman, the sandy treasures still find their way into my pockets.

My youngest also fills his pockets and spaces with treasures, though his collections look different from mine. On his carefully curated bedroom shelf, he has placed Halloween pumpkins, plastic dinosaurs, Christmas globes, pinecones, whittled sticks, porcelain birds, acorns, and seeds that spill their cotton in lidded jars.

He's gathered stacks of wrinkled papers, held too tight by eager strokes of thick paint, and a shrine of trophies—Lego creations, broken rocks, and lumps of clay—all attesting to the truth he sees. A ceramic Jesus watches over all.

As amateurs, my son and I are the less sophisticated versions of our more professional counterparts who have supplied natural history collections in museums and universities the world over. The experts gather specimens from the beautiful to the outrageous. From eggshells to fossilized sponges, their drawers and shelves brim with curated treasures. From these collections emerges diverse understanding about change over time, genetic diversity, and the effect of environmental degradation. As a once-upon-a-time biology teacher who loves the earth's richly diverse varieties of life, these insights are particularly meaningful to me.

In much the same way, I walk through life gathering moments, stories, thoughts, art, and insights that speak to me of grace. Though I love each piece in my collection, none individually is *the truth,* the big boss with the final say. Rather, each piece adds something unique to the whole, and beauty has emerged from the scattered collection. I'm drawn to moments where the spiritual and physical collide, where heaven breaks through to earth.

One such moment is a memory—set on a winding mountain road in Costa Rica when I was floored by grace. I took a mental picture because I had neither a camera nor the words.

Around a bend, the canyon walls suddenly grew to stories-high cliffs. But unlike the burnt reds and grays painting the rocky cliffs of my home, these cliffs were covered in rich green, alive with a reckless, untamed barrage of roping vines and thick, waxy leaves like hanging umbrellas. From the base of the canyon to the top, on either side of our car, the tropical walls towered, breathing steam and energy. We were enveloped in this haven—this ecosystem teeming with life. I embraced it. The scene was truly magnificent—absolutely holy.

At the time, I didn't call this experience *grace.* It was simply a moment of utter awe, distinct in essence from similar experiences to which I'd given other names—moments I've felt the Spirit, or intense love for the warm weight of a newborn asleep on my chest, or awed gratitude for the friend who showed up.

But just as I learned that all life—from snap peas to oysters—is made of the same genetic currency, I've gradually come to understand that all grace is simply godly currency. This is not to say grace is a mere transactional exchange, but more like a reciprocal gift-giving between humanity and divinity. It's the stuff that undergirds all the moments where our Heavenly Parents peek through the curtains, and we peek back—when our lives merge with Theirs. Where relationship binds us. Grace is divine help gifting us with joy, power, love, peace, hope, and everything good. But it's not just a gift given to a passive recipient; rather, we open and appreciate the gift, and then put it to work. God gives, and we take hold. Grace is our participation in the divine. Our partnership.

Grace is not, like I used to think, merely the thing that gets our broken selves into a future heaven despite our inadequate efforts. It's the thing that brings heaven into our earth right now, the thing that exists in front of our eyes, and which, because we're constrained by blinders, we frequently fail to see. It's what reaches through the murky fuzziness, the veiled separateness, between us and God, between heaven and earth. Often, it's both unexpected and unmerited.

The realization that all those seemingly disparate moments were simply grace has led me to curate a collection. I'd like to expand my stories to include the grace I missed the first time around. I hope to see those moments for what they are—to recognize them in my people and in the places I immerse myself.

Another piece in my collection emerged as I was preparing a Sunday School lesson on Romans. I was contemplating Paul's teachings on grace as thoughtfully expounded by the philosopher Adam Miller and meditating on Ashley Mae Hoiland's beautiful poetic imagery on seeking God.[1] And all these thoughts were taking root while I sat with my family near a glistening stream up American Fork Canyon, enjoying the smells of pine and soil. There I imagined a bird learning to fly—seeds for my parable on grace.

As was the case for my bird, the subtleties and fulness of each moment, person, and material often lay hidden in plain sight. Air is just air, until it's more. What to one person is a mere block of wood, to a sculptor is a boy with a fishing pole. And through engagement in the artistic process, the work of art, in turn, reveals the artist. The creation reveals the creator; they are inextricably bound.

A pantry shelf is a feast to a chef; a drop of lake water is a dynamic world to a microbiologist; sheet music is a symphony to a violinist; a verse from Exodus is a burning bush to a rabbi; a child is the most precious being in the universe to her mother. And empty sky is utter freedom to a bird.

Each person can embrace grace as it manifests in their own spheres. All of us are in practice. In learning to embrace grace, ordinary people, moments, and material reveal themselves in their extraordinariness. And we too are revealed through this gracing.

Grace appears, among other forms, as healing amidst suffering, sure-footedness on a murky path, joy amid mundane tasks, and strength despite perpetually poor habits that are seemingly unbreakable. But grace also shows up in almost scandalously ordinary moments—a conversation, a glance, a tune, a hurried day, a breath.

While grace often seems elusive, we sometimes observe those who seem to be immersed in its embrace. They make it all look so easy, so carefree. We watch to see what they do, what they know. From our external view, we see them pray, work, and serve their neighbors, all with a kind of finely tuned power.

So, whether from desperation or hope, we get to work, flapping our wings, so to speak. We give ourselves lists of all we need to do. We wake up earlier, go to bed later. Work harder. Work smarter. We are unfailingly diligent—reading, praying, serving, striving, saying yes.

But at the end of the day, we land on our rump. We are exhausted, lamenting because we can't keep it all up. Like Isaiah, "we wait for light, but behold obscurity; for brightness, but we walk in darkness. We grope for the wall like the blind, and we grope as if we had no eyes: we stumble at noonday as in the night" (Isa. 59:9–10).

But then at last, one day, doing nothing special, just walking down the sidewalk, we take a breath.

A deep one, like a yawn that opens us from the inside.

A stillness settles over us.

A calm.

We notice a lone crocus reaching up through a crusted bit of snow; we hear the wind in the cottonwoods and feel the exhale of cool winter across our face.

And in a moment, something distills in a way that transcends words.

And we understand.

Grace is not something we work ourselves ragged for. It's not a prize we earn only after a lifetime of striving—of clawing and crawling our way to the promised heavenly gates.

No, grace is already here.

It's so simple, really—just air.

It's present in the nooks and crannies of our lives, available and inviting. The hidden forms suddenly leap into view; we wonder how we could have missed it before.

It's in our lungs that fill with air. In the radiant sunshine that finally breaks through the abysmal winter. It's in the warm aliveness of the earth, its stubborn ability to send life through cracks in the cold. It's in our step—the strength of the muscles, bones, and breath that move our bodies forward—and in the sigh that dissolves the tension in our shoulders. It's smaller than we thought, yet also so much bigger. It's in the memory of every spring that somehow came, and the hope of every spring that will always come.

And once seen, that grace infuses us with life. Empowered, we face our problems and questions with a lively hope. No longer working to earn our salvation, we wake up and live in it.

Our efforts didn't open the door for grace. We didn't need to work or qualify for it. Like a bird, we just needed to fly in it. And once we did, life became what it was always meant to be—

not a race,

not a game,

not a test,

just presence in grace,

working, playing, and resting in its flow.

Language comes up short and lacks a suitable name for this way of being. I'll call it gracing. As a noun, *grace* calls up a gift from God to us. It's a thing with heft and substance.

Gracing, on the other hand, is a verb. It's movement. Flow. It's action or being—something we do or how we exist within divine relationship. It's our acceptance of the freely given gift. Beyond the common usage of the word as an adornment or garnish, I'm expanding the definition to refer to the main dish of a life lived well. Whether it's specializing, playing, or transforming, it's a way of living with God in the world.

It's collaboration.

Participation in the divine.

As for this book, it's nothing more than my collection of seashells, representing a few ways gracing shows up. I have curated my collection through the lens of one who loves faith, science, and motherhood, and enjoys exploring how they play out in my ordinary life. My collection, in turn, has formed me. I hope my reflections will point you toward your own gracing.

Throughout my life and into the next, my collection will travel with me.

And maybe, hidden in my pocket, I'll bring along one or two stowaway shells.

Specializing

We all start out no bigger than the period at the end of this sentence.

Look at it. That was us.

Just tiny specks holding tiny libraries with all the instructions for building two-legged creatures that hug, cook, and jump out of airplanes. From this one wee cell, the dot begins to copy itself—2, 4, 8, 16—each new cell emerging from the others to become no more than a miniscule raspberry.

But now these cells begin to diverge. Each holds a copy of the entire library, the human genome, but now starts to focus—to specialize. The workers in the various cells pull out books from the figurative library's first floor, second floor, or third. They use the instructions to build a three-layered pancake stack—an ectoderm, a mesoderm, and an endoderm. And from there, the little creature goes gangbusters.

A mere ten weeks after the sperm and egg have merged, the tiny being has optic cells capable of harnessing light, cardiac cells that pulse, delicate fingernails, and an alien face. Bone cells, anything but lifeless and inert, build and shape scaffolding for the amorphous mass we would otherwise become. Energy-hungry muscle cells, insulin-growing pancreas cells, and meaning-making brain cells: all these develop from that one tiny speck. And all are enclosed in a delicate, transparent wrapping of skin.

What if I was just one of those cells—one person with something specific to offer and a certain perspective of the whole? Paul thought about this in terms of the body of Christ: "For as the body is one, and hath many members, and all the members of that one body, being many, are one body: so also is Christ" (1 Cor. 12:12).

When it comes to my fellow humans in Christ, I'm like one cell within one body.

In The Church of Jesus Christ of Latter-day Saints, at least, I wonder if we sometimes limit our application of the body of Christ idea to our callings within the Church. I hear it said that bishops are no more important than librarians or Primary teachers. Which is true, but maybe we should think more expansively, in terms of our individual vocations—those pursuits and ways of being to which we feel called, based on our unique life experiences, opportunities, and interests. Specializing our lives in this way seems to me a manifestation of gracing.

Casey, ⸫ a no-nonsense mentor, gives tough love to struggling youth in both informal and formal ways. Sarah, who suffers from

⸫   Names in this chapter have been changed.

lupus and diabetes, makes it a priority to reserve her strength to be present and undistracted when her young children return home from school. Jessie serves—always doing the quiet, behind-the-scenes neighborhood work of moving the Happy Birthday sign from yard to yard during her morning walks. Mark travels the world with his family, eating with Moroccans and exploring tropical rainforests. Amanda, a professor, is intelligent and thoughtful—with her, conversations are always engaging.

And even within the realm of Church callings, our offerings are unique. Lauren was initially overwhelmed at being called as Relief Society president, panicking as she envisioned herself carting a wheelbarrow full of cleaning supplies and lasagnas through the neighborhood. Later she found grace in recognizing that her brand of love looked different but was no less valuable. The way she sat on my couch, listening with her whole body, was a beautiful form of love. No doubt she showed up for others in this way too.

The body of Christ has comedians and dancers, activists and healers, politicians and painters, musicians and athletes, those who cherish the good and those who root out the bad. There are thinkers and doers, speakers and listeners, teachers and learners, people who have found grace and those who are still seeking it. In my ideal conglomerate self, I would be all these things. But my life is embodied, not ideal—lived out with a particular personality, body, and mind. In choosing one life, one way of being in the world, I don't need to assume my work matters less than others. I also don't need to judge my friends for not choosing the life I have.

In the body of Christ, Casey is a foot, Mark an eye, Sarah a shoulder, Lauren a neck. My friends are elbows, ears, hearts, wombs, and backs. Part of choosing a certain devoted life involves un-choosing other devoted lives. It means appreciating and supporting other vocations and ways of being that look vastly different from our own.

My own choice, my life on paper, is unremarkable. I grew up with dedicated and thoughtful parents, in a house in Provo, Utah, where as a six-year-old, I took writing lessons for a short while from one of my dad's BYU graduate students. With her, I learned to write silly sentences like, "your feet are made out of chicken noodle soup," and "I'm an angel sitting on top of your nose."

Before first grade, I was warned by my older brother's friends that Miss Hamilton pulled kids' hair. I think I had nightmares before school started. But Miss Hamilton was nice, with black hair and rosy cheeks. She was like Snow White, and she wrote me a letter telling me she liked my writing.

Outside of school, I played Barbies at my friend's house since I wasn't allowed to have them at home. We rode bikes together around the neighborhood and gave names to all the houses in our little world. I took violin lessons, though being somewhat shy, I didn't enjoy performing and would have preferred doing something in the background. But eventually I learned to love a particular *Aria* by Bach. And his *Arioso.*

Every summer my family vacationed in California, collecting shells and splashing in the ocean. And I always knew my parents loved me.

I went to high school and, inspired by my dedicated science teachers, eventually pursued degrees at Brigham Young University in both human biology and biological science education. I married my high school sweetheart and taught biology for a very brief time while my daughter was a baby. Soon after,

I chose the world-altering life of full-time motherhood, and I un-chose professional teaching.

Once, in adjusting to the quiet isolation of first-time motherhood, I became obsessed with a poorly written, embarrassingly wretched soap opera that aired during my daughter's mid-morning nursing sessions. I think it involved portals to hell via the basement. I confessed this hidden indiscretion years later to my husband, who laughed with me. But looking back, I realize I was cradling a fleeting gift during those nursing sessions, as ephemeral as the flaming edge of the morning sun unzipping itself from the horizon. Distracted, I blinked and it was gone.

But time and again, interspersed throughout the times I wasn't paying attention, I remembered to seek God in motherhood. Praying looked like cleaning vomit from sick toddlers' faces, making dinner yet again, and trying to follow lively descriptions of video game levels. Prayer was balancing advice with listening, rules with flexibility, and welcoming joy. Despite the many hiccups, I have loved and been loved.

Grace has sustained me.

As my children grow and are beginning to leave home, I'm trying to find my footing in the world. I find myself with more time and desire to expand my contributions. Chronic illness prevents me from contributing in the ways I would like—holding full-time jobs and healing all the people and ridding the world of bad guys and whatnot—though my desire remains to live an actively engaged, useful, and meaningful life. Because my life is slower, and I have quiet moments to sit inside my head, I have turned to reading and writing, and I have found grace there.

Reading shows me what grace looks like outside my own sphere. Gifted writers, using words as medium for their art, invite me again and again to see. "It has seemed to me," writes Marilynne Robinson, that sometimes "the Lord breathes on this poor gray ember of Creation and it turns to radiance—for a moment or a year or the span of a life. And then it sinks back into itself again, and to look at it no one would know it had anything to do with fire, or light. . . . Whenever you turn your eyes the world can shine like transfiguration. You don't have to bring a thing to it except a little willingness to see."[1]

Or from Annie Dillard, who watched a mockingbird on the ledge atop a four-story building, witnessing as he "took a single step into the air and dropped. His wings were still folded against his sides," Dillard wrote,

> as though he were singing from a limb and not falling, accelerating thirty-two feet per second [squared], through empty air. Just a breath before he would have been dashed to the ground, he unfurled his wings with exact, deliberate care, revealing the broad bars of white, spread his elegant, white-banded tail, and so floated onto the grass. I had just rounded a corner when his insouciant step caught my eye; there was no one else in sight. The fact of his free fall was like the old philosophical conundrum about the tree that falls in the forest. The answer must be, I think, that beauty and grace are performed whether or not we will or sense them. The least we can do is try to be there.[2]

In trying to be there, I seek words to express my own moments of shining transfiguration. I am invited to both find and illuminate God. When writing, I feel the grace bodily, right here in the center of my chest—it feels like a yoga stretch, exposed and all-in, completely engaged in my offering. God is here, as real and present as a mockingbird in free fall. Wrangling words from vague thoughts is hard work, but in the meantime God shines here—transforms me here. I am powerfully drawn to participate.

"I had been my whole life a bell," writes Dillard, "and never knew it until at the moment I was lifted and struck."[3]

I am told that God is eternal, alpha and omega, the beginning and the end. It's too big to wrap my head around. Instead, my experience with God is this: I sit here in one corner of the body of Christ, on a secondhand brown leather couch, where window light casts rows of bright rectangles onto the bamboo floor. Wrapped in my grandma's old afghan, I hear the stunted wall clock tick perpetually at five minutes till six. And I write.

And here my bell is struck.

Here as I write, the previously unseen air lifts me in flight.

There are near infinite places to find God, but we can't be in all the places at once. Even Jesus didn't heal all infirmities or challenge every injustice or stretch the limits of human athleticism or create all the beautiful works of art. He existed in a certain time, in a certain place, and gave a specific offering only He could give.

If the body of Christ was all elbows, it would be, well, all elbows. And if the body of Christ was all Mother Teresas, where would be the Jane Goodalls, the Mahatma Gandhis, the Eva Cassidys, the Leonardo da Vincis, my daughter and my mother? "Good, as it ripens," wrote C. S. Lewis, "becomes continually more different not only from evil but from other good."[4] That's a fantastic idea—perfection doesn't lead to a convergence into one same way of being, but a divergence into many good ways of being.

With so many ways of being and so many varieties of work, all good work can be holy work, as the Anglican priest Tish Harrison Warren points out. This was one of the revolutionary ideas of the Protestant Reformation, which "toppled a vocational hierarchy that had placed monks, nuns, and priests at the top and everyone else below. The Reformers taught that a farmer may worship God by being a good farmer and that a parent changing diapers could be as near to Jesus as the pope."[5]

Warren explores "vocational holiness," the idea that we're actually sanctified through our vocation, which may be a job we hold, a way we serve, or a calling we hear in our hearts. "Christian holiness is not a free-floating goodness removed from the world, a few feet above the ground," Warren writes. "It is specific and, in some sense, tailored to who we particularly are. We grow in holiness in the honing of our specific vocation. We can't be holy in the abstract. Instead we become a holy blacksmith or a holy mother or a holy physician or a holy systems analyst."[6]

In other words, whatever our good work happens to be, whatever our specialty, we can find God in it. We can find grace there. Or, as one character in the film *Chariots of Fire* puts it, "You can praise the Lord by peeling a spud if you peel it to perfection."[7]

One of my favorite lines from the same movie comes from the Scottish runner Eric Liddell, who is explaining to his sister why he can't devote all his energy to missionary work. He tells her, "I believe God made me for a purpose . . . but He also made me fast. And when I run, I feel his pleasure."[8] Liddell pursues excellence in running because when he does, He feels God in the work. My cross-country-running sons have a similar perspective, one that I never expect to have because running to me feels like torture. But I am happy that, for them, it is a grace.

Or for Robin Wall Kimmerer, the Native American botanist, grace emerges from a patch of *Mnium insigne,* a wet cushion of moss most of us would crush without a second thought. Watching closely and expertly, Kimmerer sees the thread-like tip of the wandering moss waving, circling, and searching in a "most unplantlike fashion," like the front half of an inchworm probing for a place to land while its hind suckered feet stay firmly rooted. Once the thread finally settles, stretching itself taut and bridging the gap between the moss leaves, she asks, "Is that not grace—to see an animal made of green light and water, a mere thread of a being who like me has gone walking in the rain?"[9]

Absolutely that's grace, as beautiful as the one who reveals it through her own gracing.

Or from another vocation, consider the gifted Indian mathematician, Srinivasa Ramanujan, for whom equations came intuitively into his mind. In a movie adaptation of his life, he said, "There are patterns in everything. The color in light, the reflections in water. . . . In math, these patterns reveal themselves in the most incredible form. It's really quite beautiful." As an expression of pure truth, Ramanujan said that an equation "expresses a thought of God."[10] For him, the pursuit of mathematical excellence for its own sake was godly.

Likewise, Dorothy Day, the Catholic journalist and activist, found God breaking in through motherhood: "If I had written the greatest book, composed the greatest symphony, painted the most beautiful painting, or carved the most exquisite figure, I could not have felt more the exalted creator than I did when they placed my child in my arms."[11]

Whether through running, writing, math, moss gazing, motherhood, or any of the myriad other ways of being in the world, a vocation lived with grace both finds God in the work and expresses God in the work. When we find the path that combines our energy, our experience, our education, and our desire, grace breaks through in ways that help us enact those callings in meaningful ways.

Ultimately, there are many cells, and many meaningful specialties. And because we all start out as one cell, no bigger than the period at the end of this sentence, and even end up as only one cell in the figurative body of Christ, it may appear that we haven't moved much. But if we consider the whole body of Christ, where all the cells are enclosed in a delicate, transparent wrapping of interconnection, it's here that we shine with transfiguration.

We are lit up and empowered by God—all the symphonies, peeled potatoes, free-fallers, clean faces, and lasagnas—bound up in collective and life-giving grace.

CHAPTER TWO

Transforming

My friend has been known to collect particular milkweed leaves. Clinging to the undersides of these leaves are small, off-white eggs, no bigger than a pencil tip. She takes them home, places them within jars and other containers, and then waits for them to hatch. After the hungry caterpillars emerge, they feast on the thick, white milk oozing from the milkweed leaves, and my friend generously shares the caterpillars with neighbors eager to witness the extraordinary monarch metamorphosis.. My children and I have been some of the lucky recipients.

The transformation is radical. The caterpillar starts as a thin eating machine, striped with yellow, white, and black. It moves like a Slinky toy, alternately expanding and contracting its various midsections—each set of legs grasping its own foothold while its mouth rhythmically clears slices of leaf, harvesting its dinner like corn on the cob. Its head pings back and forth like a typewriter. In searching for new landing spots, the caterpillar arches its back in an upward dog yoga pose, then gently stirs the air with its head while its antennae flit around—searching.

Eventually, after becoming sufficiently and uncomfortably plump, the caterpillar climbs to the top of our kid-friendly butterfly enclosure, where it spins a sticky silk pad into which it wriggles and twists its rear end to firmly attach itself. Now upside down, it hangs suspended like an acrobat preparing for a marvelous trick. Its body swoons, settling gently into a curved "J."

At this point, the caterpillar essentially unzips its outer skin, shedding it to reveal a pale green inner skin, or chrysalis, inside. Contrary to popular belief, the chrysalis is not like a sleeping bag the caterpillar builds around itself. Rather, it's part of the caterpillar's own body—like a deeper layer of skin. Throughout this shedding process, the caterpillar wriggles and twitches and heaves, looking very much like my swaddled babies, restless before sleep.

Soon, however, the chrysalis relaxes and stills. If we could peer inside, we would see the tissues of the caterpillar essentially liquefy. The caterpillar is basically digested into a chunky bug soup. Along with a few portions of muscle and other tissue, some small bundles of cells, called imaginal discs, remain intact. These undifferentiated cells were present, but dormant, in the caterpillar. But now they are given the green light and grow rapidly into the legs, body, eyes, antennae, and wings of the developing butterfly. The body is assembled using building blocks from the bug juice. It's an astounding process, as radical as if humans were unzipped, then slowly digested in a sack, leaving inner gravel-sized pellets intact, and from which albatrosses grew from the same genetic code.

After one or two weeks, the pale green chrysalis becomes transparent, and the black and orange wings and wriggling limbs become visible inside—like a baby who is newly delivered inside a miraculously undamaged amniotic sack. The clear casing fissures, like an opening bud, and the monarch crawls out, crinkled and wet. Its straw-like proboscis flexes and extends, readying itself to feed.

After our butterfly is born, my children place orange slices in the enclosure and watch the butterfly slurp up the juice. The butterfly's wings harden as blood-like hemolymph fills the flaccid wing veins.

We take the enclosure outside and unzip the exit door. Like a gangly newborn giraffe, our butterfly awkwardly starts and stops and flutters against the enclosure until it finds the opening, then dances its way out into the sunshine. It has gone from Slinky to bug soup to flying flower—taking flight alongside the fledgling bird. Who would have thought?

All this has me thinking about transformations—the radical, revolutionary kinds that turn the world upside down, disorient and then reorient, and birth mind-altering ways of being in the world. I don't think these transformations are confined to butterflies. And I do think they highlight yet another way we enter the flow of grace.

As a child, I went to Primary on Sundays and school on weekdays, and in my mind there was a seamless unity between them. Like the caterpillar, my job was simple: consume all I could. But no one told me about separation of church and state. Sure, I attended school and church in different buildings, but in both there were simply different big people teaching me about how the same world worked.

In second grade, I entered the Reflections contest with an essay I called "Zion Is My Dream." My seven-year-old self told of a place where animal and botanical science, scriptural images, rules of right and wrong, and childhood fears and hopes all melded together in my most plausible description of a reality to come.

> Zion is the place where you can go if you are good. Children and lions will play together and the lions will do no harm. You can also touch a poisonous snake and it won't do any harm. We will not have meat because we will let the animals go free. Animals or people will not get sick, and I don't think we will have to kill animals because they won't get sick. Jesus and Heavenly Father will not let the bad people come to Zion. Anybody under eight and not eight will come to Zion for sure. And if you are eight or older and you have been good you can come to Zion. There will be peace and quiet because there will be no bad people.

> What I think Zion will be like is, I think it's a big city. I think it will be prettier than here. I think it will have flowers and trees and pretty gardens and no weeds. I don't think anybody will have bad dreams and if we did have bad dreams we would not have to be scared because they could not come true. Only the good people will be there.

> We have to be better and then Heavenly Father will bring Zion and then we can go to Zion if we are good. . . . We can help our mothers and fathers, and be polite, and don't fight and quarrel with our brothers and sisters. And bad people can be better and not kidnap and steal and drop bombs and lie.

> I like Zion. It's my favorite city. I can not think of any better.

I love my childhood certainty and earnest attempts at meaning-making. Something happened to my story, though, as I grew. My worldview fissured. I outgrew the simplicity of my caterpillar body, and my picture started to dissolve.

In high school, there were two separate satellite buildings on the south end of campus. One was the science wing, and the other was the seminary wing. As I understood it, the teachers in these buildings were no longer giving me different pieces of the same story. They were giving me completely different stories altogether, and my responsibility became choosing which version of reality was correct. Also, somewhere along the line I learned about separation of church and state, and it dawned on me that not only was it up to me to choose, but I couldn't put my teachers in the same room to show me how to navigate the dissonance.

In the seminary wing, I learned about the seven-day creation and about Adam and Eve. There was a rib. And a serpent and a tree containing knowledge of good and evil. An ark kept *some* animals safe from the flood, but the God-initiated flood killed all the rest. I learned how Christ came to earth to redeem all the evil and suffering of this broken world. I learned that the arc of the world was moving towards millennial glory. Towards unity and Zion.

In the science wing, I learned about the random nature of genetics. About arbitrary mutations that propelled evolution forward. I was taught about the divisions of the living world and what separated life into plants, animals, fungi, and bacteria. I learned about cataclysmic mass extinctions. I learned about Neanderthals and Cro-Magnons and what made these human-like but also animal-like beings distinct from us. This divergence of life had been going on for billions of years, and in the science wing I don't remember learning where it was all going, unless it was to eventual self-destruction.

As for my place in both of these stories, the seminary version taught me about being an agent of good, and that choosing to follow the laws of the gospel would keep me on the path towards God. The science version, on the other hand, focused more on caring for creation in the present. Life would unfold whether or not I had anything to say about it, and the laws of morality would keep me in right relationship to the creatures in my earthly home.

During this time, I don't remember being particularly angry or distraught about the conflicting stories. That was not my nature. I don't remember openly challenging my teachers. But I was introspective and seeking. My childhood certainty was being dissolved into bug soup, and that was confusing. But still, something like a chrysalis wrapped itself around me and held me close. Some part of me remained intact while I hung there, rooted to some unknown grace.

At Brigham Young University, I was grateful to have the science and religious wings finally merge under one roof. A physics professor became my favorite religion professor. In his

Book of Mormon class, he took all the rules, laws, command-ments, and diverse books of scripture and funneled them through a sieve in my mind. At the bottom, what came out was not unlike $e=mc^2$—but instead of revealing the relationship between energy and mass, it revealed the relationship between religion and my life. Over and over, he returned religion's list of to-dos to the foundational doctrine of Christ: faith, repentance, baptism, the Holy Ghost, and enduring to the end. It was a roadmap. A framework to make sense of all the steps. Complexity converged into simplicity.

Another professor, an evolutionary biologist, was also a favor-ite. He asked questions that broke down even more of my para-digms. If the flood was worldwide, how did Noah get the marsu-pial mammals back to Australia after landing on Mount Ararat? Why did modern-day prophetic counsel on birth control change so drastically over time? If lions will no longer hunt prey in some utopian future, what will happen to their teeth, which are opti-mally designed for tearing flesh? If gender is eternal, what does that mean for a girl who looks female, believes herself female, and then at puberty when her body fails to develop, learns her chromosomes are XY—genetically male? Is God just playing games with us?

Under this professor, more of my simplicity unraveled. He never seemed to definitively answer the questions, which, though frustrating, helped me become more at ease with ambiguity.

Over time, and in particular as I started a family, the con-flict between science and religion moved to the background of my mind. But the questions never disappeared entirely, and I'd find that every now and then the topic would resurface and

I'd discover something had shifted inside me. My concerns had settled as my awareness of the world had moved.

For one, an understanding of prophets as ordinary flawed human beings, constrained by their language and worldviews, helped manage some of my expectations. After giving myself permission to reach different conclusions than what some authorities said, I discovered an expansion of intellectual and spiritual freedom. This led me to previously untapped sources of knowledge.

I learned to see scripture not as downloaded dictation from heaven, but as a record of people not too unlike myself who were seeking God from the confines of their limited paradigms. Its pages contained both humanity and divinity, and inspired text did not deny either.

I learned to see metaphor and symbolism not as dumbed-down versions of the real thing, but as the only language capable of shedding light on transcendent realities. Sometimes fiction reveals more truth than nonfiction can. Affirming that something was true did not necessarily mean it was historically accurate. These shifts allowed me to see evolution as the means of creation not only for plants and nonhuman animals, but for humans as well. And I could simultaneously appreciate the truth of biblical epics showing God breathing life into humanity.

As the chemist John Lewis noted, science and religion allow us to see the world through our two different eyes. If you close one eye, you have one view. And if you close the other, you have an alternate perspective. But with both eyes open, a three-dimensional picture emerges that no single eye on its own could perceive.[1] My seven-year-old self may have had it right all along— it's all one story.

And so I was gradually reassembled from the chunky bug soup. Legs and wings were formed from the broth, opening me to alternate vantage points and expanded ways of being. Certainly I have plenty of unresolved questions, and many of my resolutions simply involve being more comfortable with not knowing. But in some ways at least, it feels like I've been gradually transformed through a process of gracing. I've broken through the enclosure, gangly and awkward and into the light.

In other ways, and with other concerns, I'm probably just naively chomping down as a caterpillar or helplessly dissolving in my chrysalis. For a lovely moment, though, I've become a flying flower. I have a new vision of Zion now, born from the simplicity of my childhood dream, its subsequent broken pieces, and its eventual reformation.

> Zion is a call. A hope. A pinprick of light in the dark. Zion is a place that gathers lambs and wolves, serpents and children, and holds a place for each. In Zion there is reciprocal care for each holy life.

> Zion is a state of mind and heart where fear, hate, and faulty judgments cease. A Zion heart is unguarded, soft, and exudes loving kindness to all her neighbors, from human, to plant, to animal, and to the earth itself. A Zion *mind* is similarly embedded in love, emanating wisdom, understanding, openness, and wonder.

> Zion people are wayfinders and wholemakers. They are bound in relationship to their creator and

creation, such that from moment to moment they witness the world revealing itself as if by a sea of glass. They answer life's call with rejoicing, equanimity, and vibrant creativity.

Zion wakes to beauty, light, and goodness. In Zion there is an energy—a force. Like gravity, it pulls us to each other and to ourselves. It knits our hearts together. All who discover Zion are welcome there. All who create Zion come home. It's where the pure in heart see God and where the fulness of reality opens to our panoramic view.

I can not think of any better.

CHAPTER THREE

Partnering

My son loves math the way other people love Christmas. It absolutely lights him up. When I ask him what he'd like for birthday or Christmas gifts, he suggests math toys like polyhedral dice or Klein bottles. In his free time, he likes to learn about theorems, unsolved problems, and mathematical applications. And once he gave a "TED Talk" to his high school English class about why math is beautiful. The patterns and implications are as aesthetically pleasing to him as they are useful. It's as if math is infused with a godly joy for him.

Math wasn't that way for me. I was good at math in the sense that my grades were good, but only because I could manipulate and memorize equations. I knew the rules but couldn't articulate the reasons behind them or explore what they could do. I lacked the ability to think about math in a way that was engaging or illuminating. Math was simply a chore and a means to an end.

There's a huge difference between my experience with math and my son's, and the distinction seems to hint at what it means to live a grace-filled life. It seems that any *work* we do, whether it be math, making dinner, or taking the sacrament, could be done my way or my son's way—in what seems like a lived partnership with God or oblivious to it.

But we're not used to talking about grace and works this way. We know there is an important connection between works and grace, but when we discuss this, we seem to be referring primarily to *religious* works, not everyday ones. They seem qualitatively different. We assume God cares about the morally and religiously oriented works we do: compassion, faith, truth telling, and service, because those are godly attributes. We also assume God cares when we don't do these things, such as when we're mired in sin. But we tend to see secular works such as math and making dinner as just necessities for living. They're not exactly critical in whether or not we're on a path towards God.

We're also not used to talking about grace in the present tense. We talk about our religious works needing to happen first, as if they were placed on a timeline as precursors to some future grace. We prove ourselves first, and then God opens the heavenly gates later.

But I wonder if we are missing something fundamental about works. Maybe a math example could help us here. Being my son's mom, my relationship to math is slowly changing. Recently, for example, I learned that algebra is fundamentally about relationships. I knew algebra was the branch of mathematics concerned with all the unknown x's, y's, and z's. I knew it lumped numbers and letters together, and I understood how to work my way through various problems.

But this new insight clarified the commonalities of algebra— the elements that all the various algebraic expressions share. For example, I can represent the relationship between my age and my sister's age by x-14=y, where x is my age and y is my sister's age. Even though our ages change through the years, she is always fourteen years younger than me. Similarly, I can notice other relationships: when the radius of a circle gets longer, the area of that circle gets bigger. And when I double my ingredients, I will have twice as many cookies. There is a relationship between energy and mass in e=mc², and between the various sides of a right triangle in a²+b²=c². Algebra articulates the relationships.

Works are similar. At their core, in their purest form, they are also about relationships. And not just any kind of relationship, but a specific kind: a partnership which I've called gracing. When lived in a certain way, works are a collaborative partnership between humanity and divinity that places our works and God's grace at the same point on the timeline. The way my son explores math occurs in tandem with the godly gift of grace, which is why his experience with math is so different from mine.

What is this way of living? The Latter-day Saint philosopher Adam Miller explores this way of life as the New Testament Paul has done. Paul exhorts us to "gather together in one all things in Christ" (Eph. 1:10). This way of life is a life *in* Christ. Miller writes,

This "in" is decisive. It's the difference between life and death. It's the difference between wanting love and being in love. Something changes when you are in love. It's not just that a new person is added to your life, one person among many. It's that this new person changes for you what it means to be alive. . . . Like being in love, living in Christ changes what it means to be alive. Living in Christ, I carry myself differently. I desire differently. I love differently. I greet pain and loss differently. I fail differently. I succeed differently. I part with the past differently. I respond to the present differently. I look to the future differently. . . . Rather than just storing up salvation for the future, life in Christ saves my life as *I'm living it.*"[1]

A life in Christ is an intimate partnership—so close that it feels like Christ is alive in our hearts. In this kind of life, our works come alive as a response to both life's giftedness and its need. We anticipate the givenness of God from moment to moment. This life calls us to internal dimensions of sacredness and outward dimensions of love.

A life lived this way is a dance. One partner's hand presses lightly upon his partner's back, and she pivots to the left. His hip leads, hers follows. Her eyes glance right, he follows. Each subtle movement is complemented by reciprocity, animated by the shared rhythm. One partner pulls back, while the other reaches forward, both breathing in tandem. A concentrated attention on every movement is complemented by a countermovement, creating a fluidity in which her movements flow into his. When the partners in this divine dance are us and God, we learn to respond to what God offers and give something in return. This reciprocity creates a kind of uninterrupted unity.

There are times that feel this way for me, as if I am intimately joined with a creative force. Writing sometimes feels this way. As does having a difficult conversation where deeply attentive listening and responding draw on the most generous interpretation of what the other person is saying. When my body was strong, I remember feeling this while riding my bike—pumping my burning legs up a steep hill while feeling fully embodied and up to the task. Sometimes it feels this way in a moment of service when there's utter self-forgetting. Motherhood can feel this way, too, as when the world contracts and the only other person on the planet is this magnificent being who grew from my body, and I know exactly how to care for her needs.

Too often, though, life is not this way. I'm ignorant of my divine partner. For example, I may be having a conversation with my son about *Minecraft.* He's explaining emeralds, chickens, and zombies and what role they play in the game. I nod as if I'm following, but my mind is elsewhere, thinking about chores and the news—everything, it seems, except my son's excitement. While I may seem to be conversing with him, I'm not really there. This thing I'm doing is devoid of real connection, asleep to the relationship. It's hollow. This is works without grace, and it's dead.

Recognizing this, I can try again. I can practice the dance steps even though I haven't yet figured out the dance. My son is again telling me about *Minecraft.* I really don't understand these games with nebulous objectives and complex rules. I'd much prefer *Tetris.* But I want to understand what he loves, so I'm listening to him tell me about pickaxes and redstones. I try to learn from this moment, to experience God in it. I ask my son how you get away from the zombies and why you are supposed to collide with sheep. I'm trying to understand him, trying to connect. But, frankly, it's confusing. I'm reaching. This is works in search of grace.

When the partnership finally comes, this is what it looks like. My son is again telling me about *Minecraft.* He shows me how to use the controllers and what I should be on the lookout for as the game progresses. I take the controllers in my hand and start moving forward, but it's hard to turn. I'm leaning my body to the right to try to get the little guy on the screen to go right. Obviously, it's not working. My son is laughing. I'm laughing. I still don't understand the appeal of this game my son loves, but I do love this creative boy. I find joy playing with him. He's a patient teacher, and love for him fills me. This is life in Christ. My efforts, my works, are a response to grace. God and I are joined in partnership at the same point of the timeline; we have learned the dance. The quality of this moment has significantly changed.

On the surface, each scenario is the same; each is just *Minecraft* with my son. But going deeper, each activity could not have a more different feel. The first is oblivious to God, the second is seeking God, and the third is in partnership with God. The third is what life *in* Christ feels like.

The partnership of this dance feels to me like salvation. Understanding this, I've stopped focusing on the Jesus who will come into my future and have started focusing on His coming into my present. The lines between a religious life and an everyday one blur. My search for a life in Christ requires a new kind of seeking and an entirely different orientation to my works. Works stop being a way to carry me into future grace and start being a way to orient me to present grace.

Consider baptism, one of the many works we do. I was baptized by my dad when I was eight years old. I have a photo of my baptism day, standing in front of the stake center with my family. With the summer sun in my face, I am smiling and squinting. I don't remember much about that day. I remember a boy in my Primary class also got baptized. And I remember the water was warm. I assume that I was pleased to be making that big step. I made a choice I didn't remotely understand. But I did it gladly.

Afterwards, I learned more about what this decision meant. I went to Primary and Young Women's. I learned about the temple and the promises we make there and how everyone would have the chance to be baptized in either this life or the next. I tried to choose the right and sometimes chose wrong. The sacrament was a way to renew the covenants I had made at baptism. These covenants, I learned, were like a two-way contract between us and God. We made promises, and God reciprocated. We lived good lives, and God would eventually welcome us home.

Many years later, though, questions arose. What was it about baptism that made some people fit for heaven and others not? Why require such a seemingly arbitrary entrance requirement for heaven? Sure, there is deep symbolism built into baptism, but wasn't it still just symbolism? It seemed that when all was said and done, God would be less interested in the symbol and more interested in the real thing—the transformed heart.

While these questions simmered, I heard a Jewish rabbi speak, and something became clear. While this rabbi was only tangentially speaking about covenants, he reframed them for me. He said that he was sometimes asked by people who were not Jewish, "What makes you so special?" The implication was, "What gives you the arrogance to call yourselves a chosen people?" Latter-day Saints could ask themselves this same question: among the billions of people who have lived on earth, why would God give this unique piece of saving information to just a few favorites? Who made us the teacher's pet?

The rabbi's response to this question was simple: God chooses those who choose Him.

This felt like a mic drop moment. It was so basic. Could it be that *this* was the essence of covenant? Fundamentally, it's not about reciprocal *duties,* but rather, reciprocal *relationship?*

And could it be that at the heart of every covenant we make is this one same truth? It's not just separate and distinct agreements made at baptism, during the sacrament, and in the temple. It's not a legal contract with pages of clauses. It's one promise. It's one choice. It's saying yes to gracing. Fundamentally, it's not making covenants (plural), it's living *in* covenant (singular). It's living *in* Christ.

Baptism is not fundamentally about keeping some people out of heaven and letting others in. The symbol is an invitation. Baptism says, "Salvation is here." Right now. Enter God's presence and start living life as it was meant to be lived. Baptism says, "In Christ, your old self has died and your new one has risen." Don't wait. Enter into the divine dance now, so that when you mourn with those who mourn, and comfort those who stand in need of comfort, you will do these things differently. You will do them in Christ.

Ordinances not only take on this new quality, but commandments do as well. They become invitations rather than condemnations. When "train up a child in the way he should go" (Prov. 22:6) is seen as a way to judge our children's inadequacies so we can help them measure up, or as a way to judge our own successes and failures, we've missed something. If instead we use commandments as invitations for living life as a participatory dance, our experience changes. "Train up a child in the way he should go" becomes an invitation to a deeper relationship with our child. The commandment becomes less about the *what* and more about the *how*.

In talking to my teenager about getting home before curfew, I may find my heart opening and see her as I once was—as a growing young woman trying to discover her voice and independence. From a place of empathy, I can temper my expectations with compassion. Maybe the curfew doesn't change, but the invitation does. Commandments invite us into communion and open the door to the hard work of love.

When we haven't quite learned this participatory dance, we can practice. When life's activities seem hollow, we can learn the steps. If we haven't figured out how to play the duet, we can learn scales. We can read scriptures without really understanding them, or minister without real connections, while being ready to pivot into the relationship when it presents itself in unexpected ways. It's the karate kid sanding the floor and waxing the car. It's going through motions, through rituals or habits, in hopes that they may lead to something good. It's the children of Israel looking to the serpent on the staff, and it's trying different parenting approaches. It's the bird flapping in imitation of the other birds. These works are a vehicle to grace. They school us in how to draw peace from conflict, clarity from heartfelt prayer, or joy from a chaotic evening bath time.

This approach moves us to more deeply evaluate our works. I'm inspired by those who have shown me how this is possible. The Anglican priest Tish Harrison Warren describes something similar in her book *Liturgy of the Ordinary*. *Liturgy* is not a word Latter-day Saints use frequently, but it refers to religious rituals and habits such as the sacrament or daily prayers. Warren explores the idea that the common daily liturgies of making our bed, brushing our teeth, or checking our email can be opportunities for practicing holiness. They can be practiced as liturgies to experience God in even the most mundane tasks.[2]

In addition to the many chore-like daily routines, a more intentional motherhood has often involved reaching for what lights my children up. With my *Minecraft*-loving son, that might mean some stumbling around in the game. With my math-loving son, that could mean learning about the Fibonacci sequence and how its mathematical patterns show up in nautilus shells and galaxies. Too often I'm cluelessly going through motherhood, not paying attention. But my experience changes when I reach for connection with my children through the things they love. I bring God into the dance.

I can also shift the way I speak about my activities. This can open me to deeper engagement. Sometimes a subtle word change can alter the way I engage. Instead of *going* to church, I could *worship* at church. Instead of being an active Church member, I could be a *practicing* member. Instead of *saying* my prayers, I could seek *communion* with God. Each of these shifts challenges me to see if I'm coming from a place of complacency, seeking, or loving engagement. It keeps me open to relationship.

When I find myself frequently thinking, "Let's get through family prayer and scriptures so we can go to bed," I can shift to a more seeking attitude: "Let's reach for some good to come from all this wrangling." As I practice, gracing sometimes emerges in the form of meaningful interactions or deepened understanding. More and more, I hope to embrace these experiences.

Life is busy, no doubt. And it can easily become a long list of empty nothings if we constantly find ourselves checked out or oblivious to our divine partner. We may think we're on our way to heaven as we do all the *right* things, but in this frame of mind, we could arrive in heaven and not even know it. All these works, even if performed exactly and by the book, will be hollow. They will fail to transform us. They won't help us fly.

Going deeper, we can repurpose our tools. Learning to bring God's music into our activities often requires practice. Our intention shifts. We say *yes* to God. We invite God into the process, even if the end result is unknowable or undefined. It's characterized by hope and seeking. It has a wholly and holy different feel.

When loving, grace-filled partnerships arise, we rejoice in the truths we have discovered with the people we love. We do good from a place of communion with God. Life here feels like the call and response of a harmonious conversation between two violins. Here we're serving or praying or playing or exploring math because those activities are intertwined with divine joy, peace, love, or power. They teem with truth, wisdom, or light. We are the bird flying, flapping our wings or soaring in the updrafts. The law is written on our innermost parts, engraved on our hearts (Jer. 31:33). We live the law in response to the crux of all the commandments: love God and love your neighbor (Matt. 22:36–40). As in Jesus's parable of the vineyard workers, we stop worrying about who has labored longer, and instead rejoice for all who have learned to live in Christ—whether that realization came early or late in the day (Matt. 20:1–16). Works performed in response to grace are an expression of our intimate connection to God and all creation. We're in partnership with God—in gracing.

My daughter's interests and activities have been different from my sons', but my interactions with her, when they have been gracing, are similarly lovely. Once, she was behind the wheel and Queen's "Bohemian Rhapsody" came on the radio. We blasted the music and sang at the top of our lungs. She knew the words, and I tried but have a terrible memory for song lyrics. The car windows were open, the wind blowing her brown curls, and my heart took a picture.

I have no memory of where we were going or where we had been. It was joy and laughter—my beautiful daughter, a ball of sunshine. The commute wasn't simply moving from point A to point B—a task to be completed while both of us were stuck in our own heads and lives. It was alive. Wholehearted. The connection with my daughter was full-on gracing.

Embracing these moments leads me to God in the here and now. In all the works I do, from math, to raising children, to taking the sacrament, to belting Queen, I can live more fully in relationship with Christ. I can stop living a severed life. I can learn that life in Christ has been the natural state of affairs all along.

We have a divine and willing partner.

And an invitation to join the dance.

CHAPTER FOUR

Creating

My children are made from the apples, hamburgers, and pumpkin pie I once consumed while eating for two. That walnut on my oatmeal became building blocks for the hypothalamus deep in my yet-to-be-born son's brain. And the milk I poured over it, a portion of his heart. That grain of oatmeal . . . well, that became a portion of his upper lip that tilted upward into that crooked smile while he slept.

All of us live in borrowed bodies, not entirely our own. My son and I are part tree, part grass, part cow, part deep-sea halibut. And even further back in time, our atoms were held in the sky as stars. All of us are just recycled, repurposed stuff—with shells of skin that separate us into distinct packages of me and you, plant and animal.

And when we die, we become like a sandcastle wiped smooth by an ocean wave—the shovels and buckets simply build again from the carcass of what was left behind.

Even the bodies with which we emerged into the world are not made from the same stuff they are now. Cells are constantly being shed and replaced. Every few days, our colon cells are replaced using the available muffins, miso soup, and peanut butter from our diets. Brain cells and egg cells stay around longer, but the lips I kiss my husband with are not the same lips he kissed on our wedding day.

And though we like to think our bathroom time is truly solitary, every day our skin and intestinal tracts are teeming with microscopic creatures—bacteria, fungi, and viruses. There are trillions running rampant. We paint them as threats, yet the vast majority are benign or even helpful, contributing to the body like flora and fauna contributing to a world.

We're each a globe—an ecosystem colonized by thousands of species. In the planet called us, scientists estimate that these microscopic microorganisms outnumber our own cells. Our person is more *them* than *us.*

Not only that, but from a certain perspective, the parts we claim as our own are not uniquely human. At some distant time in our evolutionary past, a cell that looked more like us likely engulfed an Archaea cell that looked more like bacteria. Together, they joined forces. This engulfed cell had its own DNA and continued to replicate independently inside its host. Our current mitochondria—the energy-creating powerhouses for all our cells—are thought to be these organisms' babies, the progeny of early engulfed Archaea. And astonishingly, they make up about 10 percent of our body weight. Considered this way, we could see ourselves as petri dishes, or microorganism nurseries—incubators raising generation after generation of little energy generators.

Even the "human" genome, the DNA inside the nuclei of our cells, is not entirely human from a certain perspective. Not only is the *homo sapiens* body borrowed and repurposed, but its DNA is as well. Scientists estimate that at least 8 percent of human DNA, for example, originated from ancient viruses through a process called horizontal gene transfer; basically, these genes were borrowed by our prehistoric ancestors from their most foreign cousins, the viruses. Our ancestors took hold of these viral genetic treasures, tucked them into their own genomes, and then proceeded with business as usual. This radical approach would be like taking some bat DNA and inserting it into our own genetic code, allowing our future children the ability to hang upside down to sleep. We're not completely human.

And after we die, despite all our efforts at embalming and preserving, we become food for armies of microorganisms. Through microbe metabolism, we eventually break down into earth, becoming elemental building blocks ready for new forms and expressions of life. As such, we are picked up by oak trees and grass, our former bodies resurrected in a way.

After considering all this, I see myself differently than I used to.

As God's unique creation, I'm more a hodgepodge than anything—a collage. Part bug, part banana, part animal instinct, a little bit of Grandma and her somewhat Roman nose, some viruses and bacteria thrown into the mix and voilà—Me!

This business of creating is not what I originally thought. I used to picture Adam and Eve developing from the dust like some kind of abracadabra magic. I imagined creation from nothing, *ex nihilo,* in a specific place and time—be it 4000 BC in the Middle East or Adam-ondi-Ahman, or two million years ago in Africa. Whenever it happened, I imagined that afterwards, God wiped His hands, wrapped it all up, and then moved on to more pressing business.

No. It seems to me now that creation is more an ongoing tinkering project, a long discovery embedded in deep time—a gathering of available resources, a repurposing of the material of the world to build new forms and new bodies. It's taken millennia for creative hands to pull together the stuff to fashion me and all my other fellow humans, not an instant. And rather than being finished, God is still in the work—a master chef, pulling from a little of this and a little of that, taking stock of ingredients from the nearby gardens, pantries, woods, and stores to add spice and flavor.

God is still creating bodies and spirits and me.

And the work and glory of divine attention creates fantastic novelty. The Trappist monk Thomas Keating illuminated this divine creativity in his poem "Out of a Stone."

Out of a Stone

Can the Creator of all lure poetry out of a stone?
Or cause a stirring of Divine Love in a human heart?

All is possible for the Creator of all,
Who loves to manifest the impossible
In endless configurations.

As the false self diminishes,
And the ego becomes a servant,
Everything turns into poetry
And everything becomes a movement of Divine Love.
But, the separate self lingers on.

Once the separate self has been laid to rest,
The Divine Presence alone remains,
And the Creator of all becomes all in all.

The silence of the Creator is thunderous,
Drowning out everything else,
And hiding in endless creativity.[1]

As children of endlessly creative Heavenly Parents, we have a birthright—the divine gift of creativity baked into our bones. Our creative possibilities, as Dieter F. Uchtdorf explained, include not just any talents that can be displayed on "a canvas or a sheet of paper." They do not solely require "a brush, a pen, or the keys of a piano." Rather, "creation means bringing into existence something that did not exist before—colorful gardens, harmonious homes, family memories, flowing laughter."[2] It's delving into the chaos, again and again, to bring shape and meaning to whatever is without form and void.

The English author Dorothy Sayers wrote that living a grace-filled life does not just involve obedience and fulfilling duties, saying *yes* or *no* or *I will* or *I will not.* Rather, it's "to be inventive, to create, to discover something new. The difference between ordinary people and saints," Sayers writes, "is not that saints fulfil the plain duties which ordinary men neglect. The things saints do have not usually occurred to ordinary people at all." The creative person answers a call: "Here is a mess, a crying evil, a need!" Sayers continues, "What can you do about it?"[3]

I've personally experienced nothing that presents more opportunities to answer this call, requiring more ingenuity and gritty creativity, than does motherhood.

In my small realm of chaos, there has been fingernail polish on the walls, a child falling from a second-story window, and dirty diapers strewn over the backyard courtesy of the dog. I've dealt with stitches and sickness, fighting and quarreling and serving the devil, exhaustion, spilled juice, broken hearts, hurt feelings, and unmet expectations. From this raw material, I can care, clean up, invite, and creatively equip my children to do the same. Each day presents novel situations in which I am called to pull from all available resources and potentialities to create something good.

Several years ago, my husband and I participated in this birthright of creativity by living in a different country. The genesis for the move was from a book my husband had read, *The Art of Non-Conformity* by Chris Guillebeau.[3] The author's goal was to visit every country in the world, and from this idea emerged our own—living for a year in another country with our family. We both agreed that while the idea held exciting possibilities, there were many hurdles. Employment was the greatest concern, yet most of Michael's work was done online. We hoped that remote work might be a viable option even though that arrangement wasn't typical for Michael's pre-COVID-19 company. Cost, the kids' schooling, and housing were also major concerns.

Yet we also imagined the possibilities of our dream—eyes opened through immersion in a new language and culture, along with unique perspectives and experiences. The idea held excitement and promise.

Finally, we began taking steps. We tightened the budget to save money, then eventually discussed the idea with Michael's employer. Amazingly, we got the go-ahead and started delving into the chaos to make it happen.

This preparation involved evaluating various locations for our adventure, investigating schooling, safety, healthcare, language, technological needs, and financial concerns. We networked, eventually connecting with a nearby family who had completed a similar adventure in Costa Rica. They connected us with a Costa Rican family who had a rental home and who were incredibly helpful in answering our many questions.

Finally, we set off with our four children, ages three, eight, eleven, and thirteen, along with some luggage and passports, to begin our adventure.

As we waited to disembark from the plane in San José, Costa Rica, I remember beaming with anticipation. *We did it! Booyah!*

Our adventure has forever etched Costa Rica in my heart. Costa Ricans have a saying: *pura vida,* meaning pure life or good life. It is simultaneously a greeting and a way of life. For us, the invitation presented opportunities to embrace the world.

Our favorite beach, *Esterillos Oeste,* was wide and warm, the margins outlined by coconut trees and loudly cawing, richly painted scarlet macaws. It was guarded by a sculpture of *La Sirena,* the mermaid. We relished the quiet expanse of sand and waves.

The road to the beach took us over Tarcoles bridge, under which at least a dozen large crocodiles always sat, fat and lazy and fearsome.

We loved a fruit stand at which we could buy cheap mangos, finger bananas, and sweet, white-fleshed pineapples, in addition to all the novelty fruits—such as pods of guaba (not to be confused with guava) that cradled black seeds carefully insulated with white, cotton-like sweetness. And we ate rambutans, the fruits we nicknamed "fuzzy guys," which taste like a hybrid of a cherry and a grape and are encased in a red, spiky, anemone-looking coat.

Once we saw a sloth, high in a tree, and laughed as it scratched its armpit in slow motion for at least several minutes. We kayaked in mangrove forests, bought strawberries en route to sulfur-spewing volcanoes, found and fed abandoned puppies, basked in a natural hot spring tucked beneath a highway overpass, and zip-lined from platform to platform over a dense rainforest canopy. We snorkeled in a shallow Panamanian heaven where light danced from anemone to coral to sponge to Dory in a scene lifted right from *Finding Nemo* or a *National Geographic* documentary.

We discovered Jesus Christ lizards—so named because they walk on water—and watched capuchin monkeys balancing on telephone wires. My favorite was hearing the sonic echoes of underwater pantropical spotted dolphins who torpedoed their muscular bodies alongside the wake of our boat.

But our adventurous creation was not simply a vacation.

We told the kids, who were enrolled in the public Spanish-speaking schools in our small mountainous town, that we could all work to learn the language and culture. And while some things were easier for Michael since he already spoke Spanish, we all floundered to some extent in what felt like a fish-out-of-water experience. It's strangely isolating to be surrounded by people talking and laughing, and only understand a word here and there. And it was odd to have an ambulance show up at the house to deliver the phone book, despite no medical emergency. We unexpectedly had no standard home address, and relied on our neighbor and his red pickup to transport our trash to the dump. As for the kids, they found it confusing to have juice served in baggies instead of cups and classmates showing up with gifts from their parents on what we did not know was *Children's Day.*

Sometimes I'd bring the kids to school, and one of their teachers would be out sick for the day, so that child's class would be canceled. Or the whole school would be canceled for reasons that were unclear.

The process of creation requires some chaos to work with, and we had plenty.

My young teenage daughter found that while most class-mates were kind and were genuinely impressed with her ability to quote lightning-fast Justin Bieber lyrics, she could only have the surface conversations about favorite music and food so many times before yearning for more meaningful connections. And the curriculum was literally foreign. One day, her agricultural class was going to decapitate chickens. This horrified her, so she went into the bathroom and hid.

Once one of my sons put up a fight about going to school, and when we arrived, he raced out of the car and disappeared down a steep hill. I called to him, but he had vanished.

One of the other mothers came to help and stayed with us during the four long hours he was missing. She spoke no English and kept saying the word *mañana,* which I knew meant *tomor-row* but later learned also meant *morning.* Maybe she was asking about what led to his vanishing act that morning. She contacted the police for us, who were on the lookout for the *little boy who didn't speak Spanish.* A van with a loudspeaker on the roof was combing the town, announcing his disappearance and asking people to be on the lookout. Neighbors and members from our small Church branch called down long driveways and over fences for him.

A woman lit a candle to the Virgin Mary for us.

Finally, we found our little runaway hiding behind a large, broad-leafed bush near the bottom of the steep hill down which he had bolted. His white button-up uniform shirt and blue slacks were muddied, and he again vehemently insisted that he didn't want to go to school.

We returned to the top of the hill, where we were met by his teacher, who reached into our old Isuzu Trooper to hug him, muddied clothes, smudged face and all. His concerned little classmates called to him by name and welcomed him from behind the chain-link fence: "Hi," they called in English. And strangers called him *mi amor*—my love.

Eventually, the chaos of school became slightly more tolerable. Our son returned to school, emboldened and more courageous. We worked on our Spanish by attending language class with Armando, a kind, elderly man I would have been happy to adopt as a grandfather. And we hired a teacher, Maria Elena, who came to our home and taught us Spanish as we sat around the kitchen table—even our preschooler painstakingly wrote Spanish words on his orange construction paper. My daughter was frequently invited by the local sister missionaries to accompany them in their work, and she practiced sharing her testimony and initiating Spanish conversations with strangers in the town square.

My personal experiences were not vastly different from those of my children, as I spent time volunteering at the preschool with my youngest. One day, tired after not having slept well the previous night and itching with bug bites, I was frustrated at not being able to communicate. I had spent the morning in a classroom apart from my son because the teachers told me he was more *tranquilo,* or calm, when I was not there. Sitting at lunch in the open-air paradise of a lunchroom, I could have burst into tears.

But then a little girl handed me a piece of her cookie. And another gave me a green grape. Everything would be okay.

We all learned better how to go with the creative flow, be inventive, and do hard things. After being called into the Primary presidency in our church's branch, I learned to teach Sharing Time in my very broken Spanish, using lots of games and visual aids. I drove a group of Relief Society sisters to a meeting in the capital, San José—in the dark, in a dense fog, along a winding mountain highway on which pedestrians appeared suddenly on the barely existent shoulder like in a terrifying, real-life video game.

Our branch members and neighbors were kind, guiding me through the farmers market, teaching me about local currency. The butcher shared *chicharrones*—fried pork—with my curly-blond son who shopped alongside me. *¡Qué lindo!*—how cute!—they would tell my little sidekick. Friends helped us navigate the medical system when our son needed rabies shots for a mild raccoon bite. They intentionally spoke slowly and clearly to help me follow conversations. They taught me to make *arroz con pollo*—rice with chicken—and invited us to dinner or to the river where we collected orchids or snacked on raw sugarcane.

When our Costa Rica time was up, we returned home and reflected on our experience. Someone asked my daughter, "Should I do something like that with my family?" She thought for a moment, then said, "Yes. Your kids will hate you at first, but then they'll be really glad you did."

All said and done, we knew that our creation was good.

And it seems to me that over the span of our lives, the sum total of all our creations may look "more like a canvas on which we paint, than a script we need to learn," as the Latter-day Saint scholars Terryl and Fiona Givens suggest.[5] Perhaps the intimidating judgment day will feel less like a final test and more like a loving God taping each of our awkward, colorful collages onto the fridge.

I suspect our individual creative undertakings are not unlike God's creative process, despite the vast difference in scope and know-how. In the beginning, we are told, God moved upon the face of the waters, divided light from darkness, brought forth herb-yielding seed, set lights in the heavens, and created great whales and winged fowl and every creeping thing, using atoms from stars as His medium. The whole process required as much aesthetic sense as technical ability. Eventually, God's children were set on the earth, with their own charge to create.

Immersed in grace, God's people would follow suit. Moses would create a people chosen by God out of a people who frequently forgot Him. Noah would create a refuge from the storm. Joseph of Egypt would create family reconciliation from estrangement. Esther would create a way to save her condemned people—as would Jesus. Isaiah would create prophetic poetry that would point to truth through all ages. And Peter and Paul would create community among a hodgepodge of Jews, Greeks, and Romans, all bound by a testimony of Jesus.

In my own sphere, I occasionally emulate my creative Heavenly Parents—the Ones who fashion their grand creations from grass, pond scum, and stars. Immersed in grace, I gather orange construction paper, green grapes, Jesus Christ lizards, and whatever else I can find, recycling and repurposing the stuff of my little universe. I create a meaningful life from a jumble of days—order from chaos, light from darkness, and beauty from ashes.

One day I hope to find it all on God's fridge—and proclaim that it was good.

CHAPTER FIVE

Teaching

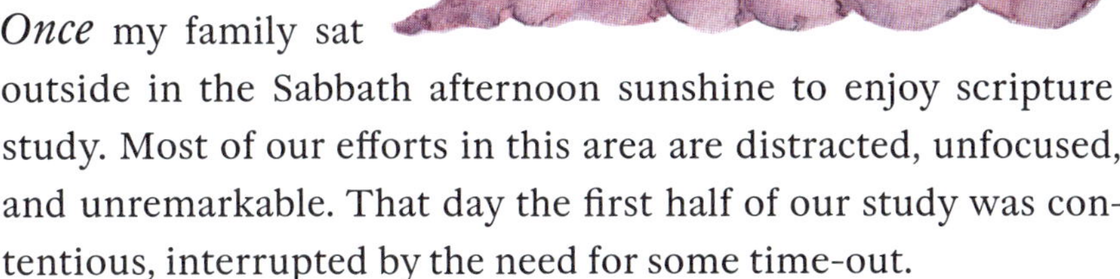

Once my family sat outside in the Sabbath afternoon sunshine to enjoy scripture study. Most of our efforts in this area are distracted, unfocused, and unremarkable. That day the first half of our study was contentious, interrupted by the need for some time-out.

Admittedly, much of our family scripture time is more of an obligation than a response to grace, and we are focused on getting it over and done. When we're more intentional, it's a practice for grace—a hope that the effort will be a vehicle for something holy. On this day, after some wrangling and struggling, our practice became an experience of gracing.

We were discussing Jesus, from the Sermon at the Temple—the Book of Mormon parallel to His New Testament Sermon on the Mount (3 Ne. 12). Sitting on the lawn, we taught the children how, over and over, Jesus says, "It has been said this, but I say this."

It has been said, don't kill. But I say, don't be angry.

It has been said, don't commit adultery. But I say, don't lust.

It has been said, love your neighbor and hate your enemy. But I say, love your enemies and do good to them that hate you.

Yet Jesus is clear that He's not dispensing with the old laws. He's not saying the command to not kill is now unimportant—as if it no longer matters what you do or don't do and all that needs to happen is to say the magic words to be saved in God's kingdom.

No, He's saying that in Him, the intent of the law is now fulfilled, or filled full. The law's whole purpose was to point to something bigger—a life led by changed hearts rather than compliance to legalistic checklists of dos and don'ts.

"What are some laws or rules in the Church?" we asked the children.

"The Word of Wisdom is one."

"Good. The Word of Wisdom has some specific rules about what to eat and not eat. And you can follow those strictly. But what is that law pointing to? What kind of person is the law hoping you will become?"

"Someone who takes care of their body."

"Yes! Someone who can do good things because their body is as strong as possible. And what is another law or rule?"

"Umm, tithing?"

"Great. And the law of tithing says that we should pay 10 percent of the money we earn to the Church. Again, what is that law pointing to? What kind of person is the law hoping we will become?"

"Someone who isn't selfish?"

"Yes, exactly. Someone who is generous and giving. That's a good kind of person to be."

We talked about how there aren't just laws at church, but that there are other types of laws: for participating in our country, our state, at school, in games and sports, and at home. Some of these we'd call commandments, but others we'd call manners, suggestions, or rules. They can all help us get along better and help everyone understand what the expectations are. Some laws, we noted, have strict penalties if we break them, while others don't.

"Let's look at some of the rules we have in our home," we suggested. "How about cleaning your room? What is that rule pointing to? Why is it helpful to have a clean room?"

"Well, when my room is clean, I don't feel as stressed."

"I'm glad you've noticed that. And I imagine it's easier to find the things you're looking for and you enjoy being in your room more."

"Yeah, that's true."

"I'm sure you don't love the rule about cleaning your room. What do you think it would take to get rid of it?"

"I don't think you would get rid of it."

"Well, think about it from my perspective. What would need to happen so that I felt it didn't matter whether we had that rule?"

"Probably if I kept it clean."

"Yes. If you saw the value in keeping it neat and organized, we wouldn't feel the need to make a rule about it. A rule would be pointless. Think about this: why do you think we have no rules about being mean to the dog? Why don't we have rules against kicking or hitting her?"

"Easy, because we're already nice to her."

"Right. You already get why it's important to be nice to Izzy, and you do it. So, there's no reason to make a written rule about it."

"Oh, so the point of the rules is to help us when we don't already know something. . . . You're not just trying to be annoying?"

Cue hallelujah chorus! And angels and confetti and dancing! Yes, my child. Yes!!

There may just as well have been a physical lightbulb turn on above my child's head. That is exactly the point of the rules. Have it written on your heart, using it as a pointer to a good life, a life led by grace and by Christ. Then the law goes away as a requirement but remains as something you want to do because that's the kind of person you have become.

Jesus is teaching that the rules point to something, but the rules aren't the point. In shifting our orientation, the law loses its bite. When the law says, "don't kill," Jesus points to "love God and love your neighbor." When Jesus says, "don't be angry," He's still pointing to "love God and love your neighbor." Look at what the law is pointing to; that's what He's teaching.

This "aha" moment was big-time grace for all of us—so meaningful and important in the context of some of our family struggles. All the subpar and contentious scripture studies were worth it for this one significant insight and mental shift. And several weeks later, as this insight sank deeper, our child commented, "I realized you are actually on my side."

Essentially this whole teaching moment was an illumination of the relationship between grace and works and between law and gospel. Living in grace is a way of orienting ourselves to God and the world. The Christian way of life seems to look at commandments not as the end-all, be-all of right and wrong, but instead as training wheels that give us some balance until we're able to ride the bike on our own.

My husband, as he ran behind our children when they were learning to ride bikes, taught them to "look where you want to go," rather than at the wobbly front wheel in front of them. Using law to look where you want to go is a much better use of law than using it as an end in itself.

The Franciscan priest Richard Rohr likens the process of learning to use commandments well to building "strong containers" that will eventually illuminate for us the "task within the task."[1] Once our containers are built, we are then able to fill them full of all the good, true, and beautiful things they were meant to hold. The containers are filled full—the laws are fulfilled.

Helping my children build strong containers and helping them understand why we're doing it in the first place means I need to toggle back and forth between law and gospel. I can't always start with gospel ("come to Christ," or "all you need is love"), just like I can't point to the invisible air and say, "look at that!" It's too abstract and invisible. It's untethered to their reality. Law helps show them what gospel looks like: tackle your room by putting all your dirty clothes in the hamper. Pay one penny for every dime.

On the other hand, if I stay too focused on law, there is the risk that my children will feel suffocated or unnecessarily constrained by it. A scene from the classic movie *A Christmas Story* illustrates this idea. It's a cold Indiana day during recess. Flick's friends have dared him to stick his tongue to a pole. After a series of double dares, double dog dares, and triple dog dares, Flick does it. And sure enough, his tongue sticks. Flick is flailing around and crying, and then the bell rings. He implores his friends for help, but his friend and the movie's protagonist, Ralphie, who is absolutely constrained by law, says, "But the bell rang!"[2] In his mind, he must go inside to the classroom and leave his friend out in the playground; there's no other reasonable option available. The bell is king. This line of Ralphie's has become a joke at our house when someone is being legalistically confined by law: "But the bell rang!"

Another risk with too much focus on law is that my children may fail to recognize that some laws *should* be challenged. Some laws do such a poor job of pointing towards a good life that a solid moral argument could be made for disobeying, revising, or eliminating them: Do as I say, not as I do. Clean your plate. No talking in the lunchroom. Girls, hide your curves. Women, submit to your husbands (Eph. 5:22). Slaves, submit to your masters (1 Pet. 2:18). Don't read ahead. Laws can be overzealous, authoritarian, misguided, or just plain dumb. And some supposedly immutable laws attributed to God have the footprints of humanity all over them. Acknowledging this opens space for flexing moral muscle and finding better ways to experience gospel.

Yet one more risk with too much focus on law is that my children may fail to discover the music behind the dance steps. If I micromanage each step, they may not discover the joy of self-motivated works. They won't discover their problem-solving capacity to, for example, find a friend to stay with Flick, go get help from a teacher, and respond in useful, loving ways. Gospel shows them that law should sometimes be stretched or even broken in service of love. Jesus understood this when he sidelined traditional laws of Sabbath and ritual cleanliness in service of others.

Ultimately, this is gospel: "Sweetheart, I would jump in front of a bus for you." And this is law: "Get out of the road!" To paraphrase from Ecclesiastes 3 (the "To every thing there is a season, and a time to every purpose under the heaven" passage), I believe there is:

A time for structure, and a time for flexibility.
A time for strictness, and a time for gentleness.
A time for rules, and a time for throwing
   rules out the window.
A time for safety, and a time for risk.
A time to let your child stumble, and
   a time to hold her hand.
A time for coloring in the lines, and a time for scribbling.
A time for broccoli, and a time for cinnamon rolls.
A time to lament "B" grades, and a time to rejoice for "D"s.
A time for Lego instruction kits, and
   a time for Lego free play.
A time for following recipes, and a time for creating them.
A time to say, "you can do better," and a
   time to say, "you're perfect."
A time to say, "be tough," and a time to kiss it better.
A time for independence, and a time for dependence.
A time to stay up late, and a time for bedtime on the dot.
A time for chores, and a time for messes.
A time for curfew, and a time for night games.
A time for "good job," and a time for "work harder."
A time to reprimand, and a time to praise.
A time to love . . . and a time to love.

These lessons are not just for my children. They're also for me. In trying to understand the interplay between grace and works, I've found several analogies to be helpful. And while all the various analogies have strengths, they also fall short. The trick, I believe, is to use the analogies to point us to what's behind the curtain. Each story tells a portion of the big picture. And we can't get so enmeshed in the analogy as to blind us to the parts the analogy legitimately fails to illuminate.

At the start of this book, I tried to explain grace through an analogy of a bird desperately trying to fly by relying only on its own resources before discovering it could simply harness the wind. My flight analogy has illuminated for me the now-ness of grace, the immediate access that's readily available for those who seek it. It shows how heaven and grace can break through to the physical, ordinary moments of life. Grace is not simply reserved for a future paradise.

The analogy also highlights for me the participatory element of grace. Grace is not something that just happens to us—being changed by a godly magic wand from a sinner to a saint. It does not merely involve our acceptance of a divine gift. Rather, it's something in which we play a part, and our participation helps to transform us.

One of my analogy's weaknesses, however, is that it misses the relational, familial aspect of grace—a parent and child, the one who loves and the beloved. I'm certain time and experience will uncover many other aspects of grace which it fails to illuminate, but for now, it is pointing me to something for which I'm reaching.

A few other analogies of grace have schooled my understanding, and for that I am grateful. And despite their weaknesses, some of which are significant and have led whole religious communities to errant views of grace, each has some value.

One analogy is a courtroom: We stand accused in a court of law. Our accuser is Satan, emboldened by a litany of our offenses. God the Father is the judge. Jesus is the advocate who pleads our case.

In this scenario, Jesus understands us. He pleads on our behalf. As the first letter of John explains it, Jesus is the propitiation for our sins—meaning that He appeases God's demands, helping us to regain favor with God (1 John 2:2).

But this doesn't mean that the *effects* of our weakness and sin are ignored, the real harm we caused to the people around us simply swept under the rug. To extend the courtroom analogy, there would be plaintiffs in the case against us, with the faces of our families and neighbors. They'd read their impact statements to the court. In very concrete ways, the people around us have been hurt by our actions and inactions.

As a mother, if I'm constantly pardoning one child's poor treatment of another, there may be mercy for the oppressor but no relief for the oppressed. And if God is constantly letting us off the hook in response to Christ's pleas, there is no justice, and the pain of our victims remains. Considering both the oppressor and the oppressed is paramount; and the process involves healing as well as pardoning.

Additionally, the work of grace does not somehow mean that Jesus is mercy personified while the Father is justice personified, and that the two are diametrically opposed to each other. After all, Jesus said that "he that hath seen me hath seen the Father" (John 14:9). This is not a "good cop, bad cop" scenario. Instead, God the Father and Jesus are one.

We should resist relegating the Father to the position of one who has set an unattainably high bar for us while Jesus covertly moves it down. Why would the Father set up elaborate systems to meet His unattainable standards, when He could just change the standards? It would be like the parents of one of my students, who, knowing that their daughter didn't earn their parentally imposed minimum "B," advocated for mercy by requesting from me a change in her grade instead of changing their own rule.

But still, Jesus offers an unearned gift. That part of the analogy, at least, seems true.

A second analogy, popular among Latter-day Saints, comes from the religious scholar Stephen Robinson. More than any-thing, Robinson's daughter wanted a bike. After saving all her pennies, she had a mere sixty-one cents. And while shopping for bicycles and seeing the price tags, she despaired at ever having enough. Her father replied, "I'll tell you what. You give me every-thing you've got and a hug and a kiss, and the bike is yours"—to which she gratefully complied.[3]

This analogy depicts Christ as a loving father who will step in and make up the difference for us after we've contributed as much as we can. Again, I believe this analogy points to truth: Jesus gives a gift we could not attain on our own. The gift brings us joy in the here and now.

But if we become too mired in the analogy, we may think that given enough time and effort, we could earn our bike or earn our exaltation. This is simply not the case. Perfection in our works does not make grace irrelevant, just as a bird flapping its wings flawlessly does not make air irrelevant.

Also, the analogy hints that Christ expects us to do some work first, and then grace will intervene. But Stephen Robinson himself acknowledges this is not how grace works. It is not simply the "cherry on top," the godly power that kicks in once we've run ourselves ragged. Or, as Adam Miller puts it, grace is "not God's backup plan." It's not "plan B."[4]

As a gift, grace is not offered merely after our inadequate attempts, but despite them. The divine gift opens a space for us to participate.

A third analogy comes from another religious scholar, Brad Wilcox. In this analogy, a mother pays the full price of piano lessons for her child. She doesn't expect the child to pay her back, nor does she expect the child to pay the teacher back. Rather, she expects the child to practice—to use the gift of piano lessons to become a proficient musician. It's not a tit-for-tat transaction; it's appreciation and implementation of a gift.[5]

In this view, grace is God's gift to help us *become* rather than to be *repaired*; it's about learning rather than earning. Practicing godliness is less about punishment or payment and more about change—about growing into godliness.

This is a needed contribution to the collection. It points to the relationship between the one who loves and the beloved. And like the parable of the bicycle, it moves beyond grace as a mere remedy for shortfall. However, it doesn't point to the now-ness of grace. As something to attain in the future, it fails to illuminate the grace in the present—the analogy would need to somehow show the joy inherent in playing the amateur "Twinkle, Twinkle Little Star," but it doesn't.

But as an analogy, we know it isn't a catch-all.

And finally, a fourth analogy comes from the Latter-day Saint physician and author Sam Brown. Brown specializes in managing blood pressure. He points out that if blood pressure is critically high, doctors will attempt to expand a patient's blood vessels and decrease fluid levels. On the other hand, if blood pressure is critically low, treatment seeks to narrow blood vessels and increase fluid levels. The cure depends very much on the diagnosis.

Similarly, Brown suggests that because the gospel includes messages of both grace and works, in determining which message to give, we first need to diagnose the problem. Since "grace raises blood pressure, while works lowers it," we'd better be astute.[6] Is the hearer trying to earn their place with God? Are they constantly feeling they are not enough? Do they struggle with scrupulosity? Perhaps they need a message of grace.

On the other hand, are they sitting back, avoiding actions that would make positive changes in their lives and bring them and their families greater joy? Are they being lazy? Rebellious? Maybe they need a message of works.

Brown's analogy points to the idea that we be aware of the learner. If the defendant in the courtroom analogy was hiding his sins, or the daughter in the bicycle analogy was spoiled and demanding, some other response would have been warranted. Teaching calls for helping individual learners who are in very different states of mind. Grace is as much about the receiver as it is about the giver.

Yet, unlike the other analogies, Brown's doesn't point to the idea that grace is a gift. It's the weakness of an analogy, but also its strength, in that it pointedly illuminates one particular portion of the sometimes-ethereal whole.

There is a real danger that analogies may misdirect us; we should be aware of how they may point us to things that aren't real. But there is also a risk in getting so bogged down by the weaknesses of these analogies that we fail to see the very relevant and transformative truths they are pointing to.

Also, there is a risk that these analogies stay abstract and academic. For me, none of them mean anything when severed from my family on the lawn. Truth doesn't exist as some high-floating abstraction outside my relationships and experiences. Only in the midst of my concrete realities do these teachings illuminate the expansive picture of grace. I need relatable teachings; I'm like my children in that way.

One day, for example, I witnessed a moment that served as a poignant analogy. It was Sunday, and I watched an elderly blind woman walk into my sister's church, white cane in hand, muscular German Shepherd at her side. The huge dog walked with almost comically tiny steps, pausing and matching the woman's slow gait—step . . . step . . . curb . . . step. Certainly, the dog could work as a vicious guard dog or an active mountain rescue dog. But following its training, this powerful, magnificent creature patiently provided eyes to a woman unable to see.

And once in the chapel, the woman took her place at the organ, no sheet music present, and played hymns from memory. She was a musician gifted and empowered by grace in the form of a trusted dog resting at her side. It was a vivid display of both the condescension and empowerment of grace. This image lifts me in the face of my own weakness and points me to grace.

Jesus, as the master pointer-to-truth, taught both the New Testament Sermon on the Mount and the Book of Mormon Sermon at the Temple.

In my life, He sits with me on the grass, surrounded by my family and friends, inviting me to see the ways grace emerges from life's stickiness.

He points me to significant details and the developing big picture.

He tells me stories, with analogies and parables, using examples that are familiar to me.

He challenges my thinking and doing—"it has been said this, but I say this."

And He guides me in making connections, as all good teaching does.

It's the Sermon on the Lawn—our daily lesson.

Attending

When I was a little girl, I remember visiting my grandparents' church in California, and someone at the pulpit expressed gratitude for belonging to the only true church. I was confused, because I thought my church—the brown brick building next door to *my* house with the detached steeple that I liked to ride my bike around—was the only true church. Surely, we couldn't both be right.

It took a few years for my cognitive dissonance to dissipate. Time and greater perspective moved me to see church as more than just the physical building I attended, and that sufficed for a while—until it didn't.

As an adult, the boundaries of *church* and the *body of Christ* have expanded even more. In my exposure to other perspectives and ways of being, through friends and books, I've seen people outside my faith tradition just as earnestly seeking grace as those within my faith. These people aren't necessarily deluded or deceived or lost, any more than I am. And working to align my public faith with my private one challenges me to live with integrity, honoring both my faith and my doubt. Sometimes that means making both my faith and doubt more visible.

For now, I've landed on the body of Christ as being not just those who belong to The Church of Jesus Christ of Latter-day Saints, nor even those who call themselves Christians. Rather, the body of Christ includes all those to whom Jesus extends His grace, and all those who receive it—all those who participate in gracing. He likely extends His grace to those who call Him by another name, or those who call His grace by another name. "Know ye not," says the Lord,

> "that there are more nations than one? Know ye not that I, the Lord your God, have created all men, and that I remember those who are upon the isles of the sea; and that I rule in the heavens above and in the earth beneath; and I bring forth my word unto the children of men, yea, even upon all the nations of the earth?" (2 Ne. 29:7)

From everything I hope about Jesus, I want to assume a larger reach over a smaller one—that He is gathering *all* the baby chicks under His wings, that He is pulling us from our root-bound pots and planting us in bigger ones. I crave an expansion of the rigid boundaries that we all draw too small.

But sometimes in trying to do this, I've gone about it all wrong.

Once, when my brother had recently left the Church, our family participated in virtual religious conversations. My brother was concerned with the "only true church" narrative, the whitewashing of our history, and the tendency to substitute works for Christ—prophets, temples, or baptism as replacements for Jesus and unnecessary intermediaries between us and Him. He disliked religious rituals such as group prayer being held up as substitutes for meaningful personal communion with God. He wasn't a fan of checklists taking the place of Jesus or works as substitutes for grace.

I believe many of his concerns were valid. But I was slow to add my voice to those valid critiques. And I didn't recognize the weight of his struggle with truth and belonging. I took the defense and he took the offense. Neither of us heard each other quickly enough. Our trust in each other waned.

As we conversed back and forth, wrestling through the weeds, ultimately, I think our relationship wasn't strong enough to handle the struggle. Tension arose, and now we just keep certain topics off the table. I don't know how to heal the divide, and it hurts.

My interactions with him felt helpful for me—in that they helped me slowly unpack my own beliefs, coming to understand the good and challenge the bad. But I didn't know how to attend to my brother's needs in a way that was helpful for *him*.

The alternative narratives replayed in my head. Maybe I could have said, "I can see how your experience of temple attendance and the sacrament was not one of grace for you." I could have tempered zeal for the truth I saw with more seeing and validating of the truth he saw. Or I simply could have said, "I don't understand, but please know I love you."

Perhaps a more attentive response was called for: "Can you tell me what it was like for you to participate in all those rituals that felt hollow? Can you tell me about what practices work well for you now?"

I didn't see how to give my brother what he needed. I tried to make it right but didn't know how. I lost a part of him, and it will take time to recover.

Sorry, Brother.

In our attempts to speak truth, bear testimony, and defend our ideals, we can alienate people. We sometimes correct when consoling is needed. Our testimony that "marriage is between a man and a woman," for example, doesn't feel like a compassionate response to someone who feels no hope of marriage in that form within the Church. Telling someone who recently lost a loved one "at least we know they are in a better place" sounds like we're being happiness bullies—so sure of our own hopeful ideology that we're not willing to sit in another's present pain. When we turn to Jesus in our anguish, has He ever responded, "Don't worry about that. Just focus on the Plan of Happiness"? Too often, we fail to mourn when it is needed.

As members of the body of Christ, there is a "time to weep, and a time to laugh. . . . a time to speak," and a "time to keep silence" (Eccl. 3:4–7).

I want to be better at weeping.

And silence.

We can learn something about this from our physical bodies. A riverway of sorts flows throughout the body, providing this mindful care. Blood vessels, the riverbeds of this system, shuttle blood to each of the trillions of cells in the body. They provide nourishment and dispose of cellular wastes everywhere they go. To reach each cell, this branching blood vessel system forks, winds, and embeds itself in and around the body's organs like an intricate tree of life. In its healthy state, the blood bathes and nourishes each cell in customized ways—by providing copious fuel for muscle cells or by sending signaling hormones to dividing bone cells.

When access to this riverway is restricted for various reasons, cells let out metabolic cries. When access is completely dammed, such as during a stroke or heart attack, the downstream cells will soon die. Whenever possible, it falls on the body to send help. It's in the body's own self-interest to do so.

My hands and feet often experience a version of this restricted flow in real-time. I suffer from Raynaud's phenomenon, a frustrating hypersensitivity of my blood vessels in response to cold or stress. Normally, blood vessels in the skin will mildly constrict in response to cold as a way to conserve body heat. With mine, though, this response is exaggerated. I could pick up a cold glass of water or grab a cold steering wheel, and my blood vessels would suddenly clamp down. Often, the blood supply shortage causes my hands or fingers to become numb and turn white, blue, or red. Sometimes I need warm water to gently reassure my blood vessels that it's okay to open up again. Pain floods my fingers and toes as the blood finds its way through.

As has been reinforced by my experience with Raynaud's, cells in the body are absolutely dependent upon an attentive flow. When cells are being suffocated by lack of nutrients or oxygen, or are injured in some way, they send chemical signals to the rest of the body as if to say, "I'm not okay!" It then falls on the rest of the body to send help. It's in the body's own self-interest to do so.

I believe this is true in the body of Christ as well. Members suffer when the flow of customized nourishment is restricted or dammed—when we fail to attend to the needs within the body. The body belongs to us all, and turning away would be as ludicrous as the eye saying to the hand, "I have no need of thee." Or "the head to the feet, I have no need of you" (1 Cor. 12:21). Understanding this, an attentive body learns to widen the flow when called upon. Attending to the needs of the body of Christ is another form of gracing. As Elder Robert M. Daines taught, to "serve in this Church is to stand in the river of God's love for His children. This Church is a work party of people with picks and shovels trying to clear the channel for the river of God's love to reach His children at the end of the row."[1]

I was just a baby in 1978, when some meaningful attention finally resulted in significant changes for Black members of the Church. Before this, I expect there was a painful tension held by many members—a belief in the basic goodness of the Church, its prophets, and its people, along with the incomprehensible restriction that Black members could not hold the priesthood or receive all their temple ordinances. Looking back, I can't imagine trying to hold both those realities simultaneously. But many did.

In the early 1970s, faithful Brazilian Church members sacrificed both money and time in building the São Paulo Temple. They did this despite knowing they would not be able to fully participate due to their Black ancestry. Other stories from Ghana and Nigeria told of faithful, converted Black men and women who joined with the Saints despite the restrictions.

Within the Church, grace finally emerged once members and leaders became deeply attentive. Living in increasing tension, more and more people were able to say, *Enough! This is not right! We know it, and God knows it!* And then the answer was so clear and right and good that it was undeniable. We weren't waiting on God; He was waiting on us to attend to each other, to be disturbed, and to care. He was waiting for us to challenge our long-held justifications for restricting the flow, and to open the floodgates with the nourishment needed to help our fellow Saints thrive. And this was just the beginning—in all the ways we've continued to fail, He still waits. He still invites. Greater grace always beckons.

Similarly, in the 1990s, President Gordon B. Hinckley had visited isolated groups of Mexican Saints—groups that had been sent to establish new areas in the decades after the pioneers arrived in Utah. Following his visit, he contemplated the decades of service and leadership these faithful members had dedicated to the Church. He pondered what could be done to help them more fully access their temple blessings.

It was at this point that the concept of smaller temples came into his mind: "I concluded we didn't need the laundry. We didn't need to rent temple clothing. We didn't need eating facilities." These were conveniences, he realized, but unnecessary for the foundational ordinances. During his return flight, he sketched the basic floor plan which later became a minimalist temple architectural plan. Essentially, he realized that the way things had traditionally been done were not valid reasons to restrict the flow. He realized it was time to "take the temple to the people." Ultimately, the seed for revelation was care.[2]

I believe that something similar is needed with our gay brothers and sisters—though I don't know what form that will take. This is what I understand: there are good people living with bodies, minds, and hearts unlike my own, who wish to live a life in Christ. Many seem to be living with profound tension, experiencing sexual identities deep importance is frequently minimized inside religious circles, while also experiencing spiritual identities as children of God that go largely unappreciated outside religious circles. And at the same time, they have powerful moral identities that call them to be agents of good. Finding wholeness and home while navigating these tensions seems a monumental task.

In my own circles, family and friends who find themselves here have tended to look outside the Church for meaning, richness, and fulfillment. In some cases, they have had to position themselves away from their own families.

As they create their paths, I wish them all the grace and beauty they can discover and look forward to positive interactions despite our differing circles. The Church is less because of their absence, and their contributions within its boundaries are missed. I believe they are still vital parts of the body of Christ, because I believe the body of Christ is larger than the Church. As the Apostle Orson F. Whitney once said, "God is using more than one people for the accomplishment of his great and marvelous work. The Latter-day Saints cannot do it all. It is too vast, too arduous, for any one people."[3] If we pigeonhole God into just one true church—one true faith tradition—we not only miss what others have to offer, but we miss what we could offer if we plumbed the depths of our own theology. As a *living* church, in the process of being restored, we are not only a work in progress, we are capable of great growth.

All religions, including mine, seem like vehicles, scaffolding, or sets of practices and experiences that can point us to grace. Some point to more truth and some point to more error, and some contain practices and teachings that speak to some hearts and minds but not others. Personally, my Church has often pointed me to grace by translating abstract principles into concrete, embodied knowing, and so in many ways it has been true for me. I've learned about "Big T" universal truth by seeing it manifest in "small t" particular truths. The vast, cosmic, unreachable God is known through the specific, Aramaic-speaking, intimate Jesus. I am pointed to Christ by a child whose pet turtle died, by a man working through a faith crisis, and by a woman skirting death at the birth of her child. Hearing the stories helps me recognize the ways grace reveals itself for others, which then invites me to see the ways it reveals itself to me. Like my childhood self, I see truth in the Church. I just understand it differently now.

I've found a piece of the simplicity "on the other side of [complexity]," as Oliver Wendell Holmes once quipped.[4] And I am also aware that outsourcing my personal faith to a church can sometimes impede rather than support my growth, so I try to be aware of that tendency and risk. As the Franciscan priest Richard Rohr pointedly noted, religion can be the "easiest place to hide from God."[5] While being aware of that possibility, I can engage in ways that allow the Church to point me and my family to grace. But I recognize this path does not work for everyone. Finding alternative practices can sometimes catalyze an earnest seeker's discovery of grace. Given this, I understand why some choose other paths.

The body of Christ seems to be made from truth-seeking members of my own faith, members of other faiths, and members of no faith—all discovering ways to participate in the divine. And our complete body is not yet healed, though I expect and anticipate that one day it will be.

Among those who *do* worship with us, there are many in pain and in need—people without traditional families or easily answerable questions. The flow of nourishment they receive has been slowed not only by barriers of sexual identity, but by barriers of language, education, poverty, neurodivergence, age, race, gender, gender identity, marital status, employment, and disability. Must we wait until the next life for Jesus to sort it all out?

For those gay family and friends who worship alongside us, I believe we can do better. When the lives of our fellow congregants look different from our own, we can cultivate a humility that loves our friends as communal fellow seekers; we can rid ourselves of any tendency to hold them at arm's length because we suspect them of being less-than. We can question any restricted flow built by our own hands and originating from our own hearts. Within our own corner of the body of Christ, we can widen the flow to send genuine love for all those with differing ways of being within our shared body. As we do this, the widened flow will also allow these cells to send their unique gifts back to the rest of the body.

In addition to this humble form of love, there also seems to be a needed form that is bold. The LDS theologian and historian B.H. Roberts showed an additional path of discipleship when he challenged Latter-day Saints to "give to the truths received a more forceful expression, and carry it beyond the earlier and cruder stages of its development."[6] It's a simultaneous commitment to true theology and dissatisfaction with incomplete theology. Because we believe that families can be together forever, is it possible that our envisioned family picture could come into clearer focus as a more forceful expression of family? Could we discover an expansive vision that includes our *whole* human family? Coming "boldly unto the throne of grace" (Heb. 4:16), we could discover a God who is bigger than we currently comprehend.

The ongoing restoration could bring about a Zion people from the full spectrum of willing participants. We could go beyond our current answers in ways that ask new questions. What is God's plan for our gay brothers and sisters—in a later heaven and in the present now? Do we have enough certainty about familial connections in the next life to warrant our certainty about this one? Could a life in Christ include moral, covenantal commitment between gay people who have chosen each other? Could this path also be paved with covenantal love and be guided by God? What helps bring our friends to Christ and what does not?

Like Moses, who had the audacity to remind God of His seeming forgetfulness towards His covenant Israel, we could plead boldly for our people (Exod. 32:7–14). Or like Abraham, who made intercession for a people God had slated to destroy, we could challenge God for the sake of our friends (Gen. 18:23–33).

There is a word derived from Hebrew, chutzpah (HOOTZ-pah), that roughly means impudence, gall, or cheekiness. In Rabbinical literature, it connotes an arrogance before God but with a positive twist—a moral audacity that challenges the status quo and imaginatively demands something better. It's holy brazenness. On behalf of our fellow Saints, we could use some chutzpah.

And where we lack good answers or questions, we could be more willing to sit in the uncertainty. Writing this chapter has made it clear to me that I often don't even have the questions, let alone the answers, for the many challenges faced by my fellow seekers. At the very least, I think we could avoid making meaning at the expense of our friends. While simple answers seem to point to simple solutions, they are often not based in reality. For example, we could claim that a depressed person could simply choose to be more positive; doing so helps us feel more secure that this undeserved fate wouldn't happen to us or our loved ones as long as we made all the right choices. We may claim that a child got low grades because he didn't study, a person is incarcerated because they broke the law, our gay friend left the Church because she was enticed by the world, or a person is sick because they didn't eat right. All of which may be true . . . but also may not be. Clearly demarcating cause and effect may help us feel better, but it can also be an excuse to withhold compassion.

Maybe a better response is at the beginning of Job's story. His friends saw a righteous man in great sorrow and were left with no reasonable response or explanation but to sit with him in ashes.

The Kingdom of Heaven, Jesus said, is within us. It's not just in a far-away celestial land where God will make everything right that is currently wrong. As cocreators with God and cobuilders of Zion, we can harness grace to intervene in the stickiness now—to merge the disparate visions of a glorious family-centered heaven with each heaven-centered human of earth's family who wants to be there. In sitting deeply in that ash-covered tension, we can embrace grace. A way forward will be clear—one that finds a place for good people both here and in the future that is grander and brighter than we can now imagine.

In the body of Christ, I am trying to listen to those who are in pain—trying to hold the tension with them, regularly failing but trying. As Thomas Wirthlin McConkie wrote,

> Establishing Zion isn't simply a matter of converting others to our way of seeing so much as more deeply converting ourselves to seeing more of the Whole. All of us are engaged in the pursuit of a meaningful life. Is our own meaning making flexible enough to include the meaning of others? Zion needs all of our perspectives in order to flourish. We can become the sons and daughters of God yet—not through a narrowing of orthodoxy, but through a multiplying of human and Divine perspectives, always more numerous than the grains of sand along the beach.[7]

Grace is not simply vertical—God reaching down and us reaching up. It's also horizontal—us reaching for God in the world, in the perspectives and experiences of others, and finding Him there. The symbol of the cross reminds us of this.

Horizontally, grace is finding God in the hand, the foot, or the eye of the body of Christ, in those who often see things differently than we do. It's moving beyond the status quo and our own voices. It's seeing Jesus in the face of the other and removing all the boundaries within ourselves to do so.

The body of Christ as a whole, healthy, living body is the beautiful reality of Zion. It relies on each specialized part, attends to the needs of each part, and in its entirety is capable of magnificence.

Redeeming

My father's mother—my Grandma Florence—was a spunky, short, Italian woman who wore purple floral muumuus and smelled of Elizabeth Taylor's *Passion* perfume. She pulled her thick, black hair, streaked with white, loosely back with bobby pins.

With a signature raspy laugh, she always made sure we had plenty to eat. She taught me that the foundation of cooking was olive oil, celery, onion, and garlic. She always knew the latest scoop about everyone in the family and was quick to send a little money to any she deemed in need.

An only child, she grew up near Hollywood, California. She was part of a large extended Italian family, whom I picture in my mind like Toula's family from *My Big Fat Greek Wedding*—large, loud, food loving, and very invested in each other. But their strong tradition of family became increasingly fractured after they immigrated to America.

When Flo was only four years old, her father, Henry, left the family for another woman. On his way out, he told his wife, Esther, that he had met a woman in Portland and would be back if the woman wasn't pregnant. He borrowed money from extended family, which he never repaid, and even took Flo's piggy bank with him.

He never returned.

Flo and Esther were left shattered, with nothing. Flo remembered her mother holding her in bed, weeping and saying, "Why did he leave us? What did I do? How am I going to take care of you?"

Esther started a small restaurant, and the mother and daughter lived in an attached bedroom and bathroom in the back. She worked long days serving roast and potatoes, burgers and sandwiches. When her responsibilities became too much, Flo went to live with extended family while Esther paid for her care and continued to serve customers. She'd complain to Flo about "that no-good father of yours."

Fast forward many years to after her mother had passed on, my Grandma Flo learned that her father had married the other woman and had raised three children with her. He stayed with his new family until his death. At one point, Flo was able to meet her half-sister, who showed her photos of their father with his new family—happy pictures like those celebrating birthday parties. Later, my elderly grandma, still wounded from her childhood loss, said, "I don't know why he didn't love me too."

As her own life was nearing its end, her son—my uncle—reminded my grandma that she would be meeting her father on the other side. He put a picture of her father on the wall, in hopes that his image would facilitate forgiveness. Early on, my grandma would walk by his picture, point her finger at her dad and give him a what for.

"Bad boy!" she would scold.

As time went on, she softened ever so slightly. While never becoming particularly warm towards him, she at least became less hostile.

I wonder how the heavenly family reunion played out.

I wonder if there is still unfinished work.

Recently I did the unthinkable. I performed temple ordinance work for Beulah Elizabeth Schultz—the other woman who stole Henry's heart away from my family. I pushed aside the sense of betrayal, as if I was condoning the harm to my family in which she was complicit. But I also had a meaningful sacred experience and felt like the work I was doing was holy—extending an olive branch of reconciliation between Florence, Esther, Henry, Beulah, and my entire family.

I have little clarity on what the whole temple experience means or what realities it brings about. But there is something powerful in the idea that remembering our dead—their suffering, their grief, their sin, their pain, their hopes, their missed opportunities—is in some way redemptive when we seek to make right what was wrong. In remembering Beulah, though we aren't closely related, maybe I am offering something on behalf of my family that my grandma is no longer able to give but which Beulah can nonetheless receive. And maybe it's not a betrayal on my part if I am simultaneously reaching for divine healing for all those harmed by this act of betrayal, both among the living and the dead. Maybe I am participating in something redemptive not just for Beulah, but also for my grandma.

I believe that is what Jesus's grace offers. And as I seek to live in similitude of Him, I believe He asks no less of me.

Redemption may be another manifestation of gracing in that it facilitates not only divine forgiveness but also divine healing. Maybe all this points to Jesus—as everything seems to do—as a wholemaker who reconnects us with God, offering unmerited gifts which facilitate healing for both receivers *and* givers of wrongs.

The priest Gregory Boyle, who worked for years with gang members in Los Angeles, highlighted this paradoxical redemptive love. He recalled the "precocious, funny, bold" Betito, only twelve years old, who was gunned down by two young men that Boyle also knew. The bullet pierced one side of Betito's abdomen and exited the other, and he died soon after a valiant surgical effort. How do I respond, Boyle asked in his grief, when "kids I love [kill] kids I love"?[1] The faces of both victims and victimizers plead for compassion.

I love Terryl and Fiona Givens's insight that *sodzo,* the Greek word translated as *savior* in the scriptures, is elsewhere translated as *healer.*[2] With equal linguistic justification, we could call Jesus not only the Savior of the World, but also the Healer of the World—healer of both hard hearts and broken hearts, of abusers and abused.

There is a need for redemption on both sides. In doing temple work, it may seem that our efforts are one-sided. Those with power are often those with records. The powerless often lack paper trails. We have records for the victors and those who were privileged enough to be buried in marked graves, while the slaves, the poor, and those who never bore children often had no one to record their names. Surely that's unjust. And in linking the human family through temple work, we run up against these incriminating realities.

Given this historical void, we could understandably give up on the temple project. But we're a stubborn people. My hunch is that someday, when science catches up to the spirit of the temple project, we will be able to read our family records not just from birth certificates, marriage records, and tombstones, but from our bodies' own genetic code. And whether we learn about our family in this way or another, there's more to the project than linking names and checking off ordinances. We're linking souls. We're welding hearts from both sides of the veil and both sides of painful conflicts. In this effort, my overarching desire is in gathering the entire human family home to each other and to God.

That's the fundamental work.

Remembering and redeeming the dead reminds us that the Atonement of Jesus applies not just to abstract everybodies, but to specific neighbors, coworkers, and family members that irk and harm us—Kathy from accounting, Greg who lives around the corner, or even Beulah. In doing work for a specific person on an actual temple card, I am reminded of the much bigger universal family of which I'm a part and in which I'm immersed—for better or worse. In doing the temple work for Beulah, I'm reminded of the healing work in which I should be engaged here and now.

At some point, I will pass on, and my children and descendants will remember the shadows of me—not just my eulogy strengths but also my sins and weaknesses, which will show up as unhealthy patterns in their lives.

My daughter, for example, was barely an adult when I asked her what I could have done better in raising her. After some thought, she suggested that I could have shown more emotion. In doing so, she could have learned better how to deal with her own turbulent emotions, especially during her teenage years.

This was illuminating and perceptive.

Her observation reminded me of my response at the emotional loss of my childhood family dog. Lady had unwittingly come across some strychnine-laced cat food placed by a teenage neighbor as bait for stray cats. The result was traumatic, tetanus-like muscle contractions and an abrupt, painful death on the veterinarian's table.

My mom wrote about the grieving aftermath. There were five of us children at the time, ranging in age from four to thirteen. The responses varied:

> My nine-year-old sister: "I feel like breaking something."
> My four-year-old brother (while hitting the table):
>   "I hate this! I hate this! I wish I could cut off my nose."
> My thirteen-year-old brother: "Oh no, oh no! I want Lady.
>   I want Lady. I want Lady back. Lady, Lady, come here,
>   Lady! Come here, Lady. . . . Was I ever mean to her?"
> My eight-year-old brother: "When I was in fights
>   with people, she'd play with me and comfort
>   me. She was so nice. . . . I'd give anything to
>   have Lady back. I'd give all my money."
> Of my own eleven-year-old response, my
>   mom wrote, "Hannah . . . didn't say much.
>   She went to her room and cried."[3]

I'm not sure why this was and often is my go-to response. On more than one occasion, I've waited until my husband has gone to sleep before ugly crying into my pillow. Or I turn my head away when tears come—or retreat. I've buried my difficult emotions, not knowing how to process or display them. It may be because I'm naturally introverted. Or because I see the fallout when I have not done this well. Or because I'm too proud. Or not proud enough.

Whatever the cause, I was unable to show my daughter how to live well with turbulence. And in her future, it's possible that I may show up in her memory as a source of her pain, an obstacle to her growth, or both.

But her memories will redeem me when her broken edges mend—when she remembers what I was unable to give and recognizes and takes hold of what she needs. It's not a matter of looking back and saying the words "I forgive you" as much as it is in enacting grace-filled ways of being in the context of her own messy, beautiful life. Redemption lifts both of us as she's ushered into the ever-present flow of transformative grace. When she finds healing and she models needed responses for those within her own stewardship, she will simultaneously reach across space and time and heal me. When my omissions no longer taint her ability to live a life of grace—one in which the whole spectrum of rich human emotions is displayed in vibrant, healthy ways—we will both be redeemed.

But certainly, this weight is not solely on her shoulders. Jesus bears it. As does the body of Christ. In all the ways my daughter and I remain broken and unfinished, others will continue the work while Christ imbues it all with meaning. Without each other, we will never be made perfect. You can't have one perfect word or one perfect note; it's only in relation to the whole poem or song that it achieves perfection. We complete each other's sentences and each other's stories. We answer each other's questions. We're part of each other and of the same body of Christ. And that whole body needs to be put right.

The work of remembering our dead reminds me that salvation isn't just an individual matter. Healing and redemption do not occur in isolation, but in collaboration—amid one giant, universal family.

I'm not sure Jesus's power is able to pardon Henry and Beulah for their adultery without also healing all those who reeled in the aftermath of that betrayal, as well as those around Henry and Beulah—the generations of family and associates who contributed to the destructive patterns of thought and behavior that led to the affair. You can't fix a tangled mess by smoothing only one strand.

As for me, Jesus will not pardon me without also healing those whom I have hurt with insensitive and sinful words, actions, and inactions. And that will all take time, and work on either side of the veil, and likely generations—much more time than I have in one life.

My children will remember me not just by the stories they tell, or the words I write, but in their bodies—their genetic history, their thought patterns, their blind spots, their language, their habits, and their knee-jerk reactions. I will show up in both the distracted and patient responses they give to their own children, in the mannerisms and expressions of their children, and in all kinds of surprising and unexpected places. Some will be good memories, some bad. But in participating in the long and patient process of redemption, all will be made right. I will bring a degree of healing to my ancestors and descendants when I make right what is wrong, and my descendants will continue the work.

This grace-filled way of remembering seems to be an integral part of redemption. It's not the type of remembering that involves witnessing some discrete, past moment, unchanged in time and space, as if you were a fly on the wall sent back in a time machine. In a spiritual sense, I believe remembering involves reworking the past, reconstructing its meaning from one of betrayal and pain to one of redemption and healing.

It's completing the unfinished and unresolved stories left hanging by estrangement and death—transforming falls into redemptions. It's *tikkun olam,* a Hebrew phrase roughly translated as repairing or healing the world.

It's Moroni remembering the egregious sins of his people, while simultaneously ushering in a more hopeful future by burying his record for future generations.

It's the early Christian disciples, who had anticipated a glorious, militaristic Davidic deliverer. But instead, they experienced a messiah who was a poor, itinerant preacher who was horrifically crucified by the very Romans He was supposed to overthrow. In the presence of that reality, they re-read and re-interpreted their cherished Hebrew scriptures in new light, discovering meaning more precious than they originally anticipated. In writing scripture about Jesus's life and ministry, they were not merely recording history but redeeming it by building meaning from their shattered expectations. The process imbued their human reality with divine hope.

This type of remembering redeems Esther, Henry, Beulah, and Florence, my daughter and me, and creates something better from all of it. It recognizes that others in the body of Christ are also on our team, and across time and space they will accomplish the things we can't.

Like the Japanese art of *kintsugi,* it's taking the broken shards of ancient pottery and rejoining them with seams of gold—taking the painful past, the sins of our fathers and mothers, and creating something meaningful and transformative. We can heal our dead and ourselves when we bring the whole of humanity to the altar of God—not as individuals, but as one massive, messy whole.

For me, the temple points to something bigger and grander than it's often given credit for. It's not just my nuclear family that can be exalted for eternity; it's the whole human family. And it's not just a ticket into heaven; it's the healing, redemption, and making right of all that is wrong in the human family—all of creation. It requires remembering all that went wrong and enacting ways to make it right. It involves immersing ourselves in the power of the divine, as well as in the reality of humanity, infused with deep time and ridiculously drawn-out patience.

Jesus shows us how this is possible. He remembers us not just in the abstract, but in His actual body: "Behold, I have graven thee upon the palms of my hands" (Isa. 49:16).

We are in His scars.

He took all our sins, pains, and sicknesses upon His body and transformed all of it. His body—the body of Christ—represents all of us who do the same.

We bear one another's burdens, say all the unsaid things, bind up all the hurts, right all the wrongs, and wipe all the tears from all the faces. We do not just what is required or deserved, but what is needed. We pick up His yoke and remember that the weight is shared among all those in the family of God who are willing, from past to present to future.

CHAPTER EIGHT

Wrestling

In the summer hills behind my maternal grandparents' home in Southern California, the earth pleads for water like lips, cracked and gaping. Yet the same baked land is home to orange trees from which my grandpa would prepare fresh-squeezed orange juice during our annual family visits. There was nothing more heavenly—like sun-kissed honey ambrosia.

Once my husband and I brought our own children for a visit. On a walk to the eucalyptus tree (or "euca-lipstick" tree, as my young cousin called it), we discovered a brutal scene.

A venomous tarantula hawk wasp, its translucent rust-colored wings held erect by gangly appendages, was dragging its prey along the dirt—an immobilized, hairy tarantula that jerked over the uneven ground like a rubber toy.

Second only to the bullet ant, the stings of these monstrous wasps are ranked most painful in the vast insect world—described by one researcher as "immediate, excruciating pain that simply shuts down one's ability to do anything, except, perhaps, scream. Mental discipline," the researcher continued, "simply does not work in these situations."[1]

But the wasp's prey of choice, the tarantula, has an even more horrifying fate than these poor souls. The female wasp wrestles with its victim, grasping it with long, hooked claws and stinging it between the legs. The tarantula is paralyzed and is then dragged by the wasp to a house of horrors—a lair in which the wasp lays a single egg on the still-living tarantula's abdomen. After hatching, the larva digs its way down into the tarantula, feeding insatiably upon it, while bypassing vital organs in order to keep its feast alive as long as possible.

On that day, I was still unaware of the notorious sting, so I unwittingly scooped the creatures up—attached predator and all—in a torn plastic water bottle and froze them next to my grandma's Eggo waffles. Once home in Utah, my son preserved them as part of his eighth-grade biology insect collection. Last I heard, both the insect predator and the arachnid prey were displayed on his biology teacher's Wall of Fame.

And the cycle of life continues.

It's relatively easy to find grace and God in some places—fresh-squeezed orange juice, mountain streams, songbirds, coral reefs, laughter, double rainbows, and tangerine sunsets. My childhood crayon drawings are proof enough for me.

But where is God in the gruesome, ugly tarantula hawk wasp burrows? Where is grace in the painful, distressing, soul-wrenching dark nights?

My evolution professor once related Charles Darwin's dark night of the soul and his transition from a Christian to an agnostic. It did not come, as many assume, solely embedded in his theory of evolution by natural selection—his competitive, dog-eat-dog world where only the fittest species survive.

Rather, some believe, it began with the death of his beloved ten-year-old daughter, Annie. Darwin wrote that his daughter had been "the joy of the Household, and the solace of our old age." Just a week after her tragic death, following months of mysterious illness, Darwin wrote of his Annie, "She must have known how we loved her; oh that she could now know how deeply, how tenderly we do still and shall ever love her dear joyous face."[2]

Darwin was too grief-stricken to even attend the funeral.

It's the age-old problem of theodicy. How can we reconcile God's providence in the face of evil and pain? Philosophers and theologians have wrestled with this question for centuries, while everyday seekers live out this wrestle time and again.

My own dark night of the soul has frequently reared its ugly head in the form of chronic illness. It began just shy of twenty years ago, when I awoke at night to use the bathroom and discovered it hurt to walk. It was as if someone had been hammering the tops of my feet in the night while I slept—some deranged little elf on a sadistic mission.

In the morning and as the day progressed, the pain would dissipate. But at night, the phantom would return for his nightly poundings. It was bizarre, because I couldn't trace the pain to an injury and because it didn't follow the predictable pattern of pain (more intense, then less, then gone). Rather, it would come and go, sometimes reappearing in a different location, sometimes increasing rather than decreasing in intensity. It was haphazard and unsettling.

Since the diagnostic protocol looked not just at lab tests or imaging but at a full clinical picture over time, it took several years to receive the eventual diagnosis: rheumatoid arthritis (RA), an autoimmune disease that frequently affects joints. In auto-immune disease, the immune system is in overdrive. It detects pollen—attack! Peanuts—attack! Any number of other benign triggers—attack! It may even be bored due to our hypersanitized world—attack! Like other autoimmune diseases, RA warps the immune system into a trigger-happy mania that causes collat-eral damage as it fights against nonexistent enemies. Detonating its arsenal against vague shadows on the wall, it leaves a broken battleground in its wake—my body. And there is no cure.

In addition to my feet, other joints became affected in the initial years—fingers, wrists, knees, and shoulders. I remember those cursed little onesie snaps during my son's nighttime diaper changes—how absurdly painful it was to pinch those snaps closed. Or lifting my arms slowly above my head to put on a shirt, wincing as my shoulders burned. Or doorknobs—those brilliant little inventions that keep young toddlers out of forbidden areas, but which at times required one hand bracing the other to ease the twisting in my throbbing wrist.

In addition to pain, there is frequently a dragging fatigue associated with autoimmune illness—as if you have ankle and arm weights as you walk through a sea of Jell-O wherever you go. Simple tasks take longer. They're harder. It feels like the day after you've had the flu, when you're achy and beat, but every day is Groundhog Day, and that day never ends.

Of course, the whole disease ebbs and flows, and some months or years are better than others. In my case, it has warped into a distinct but related autoimmune disease called scleroderma. Whereas rheumatoid arthritis frequently attacks joints, scleroderma targets the skin. The name *scleroderma* means "thick skin," which describes the thickened skin that affects many sufferers. But like rheumatoid arthritis, scleroderma causes pain and fatigue. It can also attack inner organs, becoming life-threatening if it decides to battle it out with organs such as the heart or lungs. It's a confusing disease both because of its varied manifestations and its uncertain course.

Lately, it's my muscles that cause me the most pain. I don't know if it's due to a different disease altogether, a side effect from medication, or an unusual manifestation of my growing list of diagnoses. It seems like a paradoxical response to pain, but many days there is nothing I would like more than that little maniacal elf to come back with his hammer and pound my muscles into oblivion. Wrestling with chronic disease often means wrestling with a language problem. I can't go to my doctor and say it hurts *here,* and then point to my whole body. I can't say, *please doc, just send me to someone who will squeeze the deep aching from my arms and legs like toothpaste. Please just fix me.*

Sometimes, in my dark nights, I pray God would swoop down and take me for a heavenly field trip—not a permanent one, mind you, but just a brief breather. Just for one day.

It's tempting to wallow in an immature self-pity—turning into myself, becoming caged with only my own suffering. But this is not who I want to be. Another inclination is to downplay my own suffering because many have it so much worse: horrific abuse, loneliness, betrayal, slavery, gnawing hunger, and violent war. Yet I also know this isn't a suffering Olympics. There are no medals for the most-wounded winners. Comparisons are counterproductive. I'm simply hoping to carry my own cross well, seeking to live a life imbued with grace.

And so, my question resurfaces. Where is God in the burrows of the gruesome, ugly tarantula hawk wasps? Where is God in chronic illness? Where is grace in the painful, distressing, soul-wrenching dark nights?

One of the unique challenges of chronic illness is its ambiguity. Most days, a person lives in a confusing no-man's-land between health and sickness. It's often a blurry place of not-quite-sick and not-quite-well.

I may show up to an evening event looking seemingly fine, but I'm able to be there because I have carefully and intentionally rationed my energy during the day. My cross is invisible. I almost never use a wheelchair; I don't limp or carry a visible marker like an oxygen mask or feeding tube. But I also don't run or even stand for long, nor do I spend long days meandering through shopping malls or amusement parks.

I'm careful—measured. Even my movements are rationed. There's a kind of carefree recklessness even in something as benign as conversation—a gesticulation of the arms, large inflections of the voice, an unpredictable expressiveness of the face. But I've found that even my conversation reflects this careful conservation. I stay closer to my body. The words are rationed and the movements smaller, slower, and more intentional.

The therapist and multiple-sclerosis sufferer Robert Shuman observed of his progressing illness that "once-simple choices about trips to the city or walks downtown become intensive, hypervigilant, body-scanning, problem-solving matters."[3] I can relate. Is there a place to sit down? Can I politely excuse myself from a conversation without it being socially awkward? What is my body needing right now—have I demanded too much of it, stretched it too far? Is my body so bossy that it will prevent me from being sufficiently focused on the social task at hand? What will this cost me later today? Tomorrow?

A few years ago, I was at a low point. Daily I felt drained from the moment I opened my eyes in the morning. Even showering felt like a monumental task—so big. So heavy. One day I switched a load of laundry in the basement and then lay down on the floor because it was too much effort to walk the half flight of stairs to the family room. Sitting upright at the table for a meal was sometimes too much. There was no relief in sight, and I had no idea how I could be a mother and wife, let alone a fulfilled human being in this body that was absolutely void of vitality. I had nothing.

My sense of spiritual connection was also at an all-time low. The gospel message was "turn to Jesus. He will not forsake you." But the invitation seemed suddenly inane, nonsensical. I felt forsaken. Utterly abandoned and forgotten by God. The chasm between what God offered and what I believed Him to be capable of offering was entirely too wide, and I found myself stranded in the gap. My arms stretched wide between two truths—the attentive God I trusted, and the absent God I experienced.

There in the dry, parched no-man's-land was my wrestle. I was Jacob, wrestling with the messenger and crying, "I will not let thee go, except thou bless me" (Gen. 32:26). I was Sarah, abandoned between promises of a numberless posterity and the reality of an empty womb (Gen. 17:16).

And time stretched on. So much time.

In hunger, I turned anew to all the things that were supposed to help me discover Jesus. My scripture study was not orderly or methodical. I clung to the words of Isaiah, which became almost a mantra for me:

> For a small moment have I forsaken thee; but with great mercies will I gather thee. In a little wrath I hid my face from thee for a moment; but with everlasting kindness will I have mercy on thee, saith the Lord thy Redeemer. (Isa. 54:7–8)

I read the promises over and over, though deep down I wondered if the words were just pretty poetry and nothing more.

> When thou passest through the waters, I will be with thee; and through the rivers, they shall not overflow thee: when thou walkest through the fire, thou shalt not be burned; neither shall the flame kindle upon thee. For I am the Lord thy God, the Holy One of Israel, thy Saviour. (Isa. 43:2–3)

My prayers were urgent, though they were largely without words. I stumbled along, doing what I could to care for myself and my family, but feeling very much a forsaken failure. My attentive husband literally carried me when I needed it and, along with family and friends, sat with me, cleaned our house, brought me dinner, and pointed me to hope. I listened to Christian hymns on repeat:

> "When peace like a river attendeth my way,
> When sorrows like sea billows roll;
> Whatever my lot, Thou hast taught me to say,
> It is well, it is well with my soul!"[4]

I practiced daily for grace. Absent experiences of grace, I clung to practices out of desperation.

> "Be thou my vision, O Lord of my heart
> Naught be all else to me, save that thou art
> Thou my best thought, by day or by night
> Waking or sleeping, thy presence, my light."[5]

One day—I can point to the exact place I stood in my bedroom, next to my Great-Grandma Esther's hand-me-down jewelry box—I was pondering some scriptural examples of unflinching faith, including the biblical Esther, who declared, "if I perish, I perish" (Esther 4:16). There were also Shadrach, Meshach, and Abed-nego, who knew that God had the ability to deliver them from the fiery furnace, but also knew that if He didn't, they would remain faithful (Dan. 3:17–18); and Mary, who with absolute submission said, "Behold the handmaid of the Lord; be it unto me according to thy word" (Luke 1:38).

And I asked myself, if I got to the point where I simply could not find the divine communion and spiritual healing I sought, what would I do? Would I give up on the Lord? Would I turn elsewhere?

Almost as I thought this, in a holy, perhaps mystical experience which I can only call gracing, I knew that I would never turn my back on the Lord. It was simultaneously a decision, a feeling, a direction, and a command. It was also a scripture and a hymn:

> *Even if I live my whole life and never find the peace I seek, I will not give up on the Lord. I will wait upon Him however long it takes.*

On the surface, these words barely touch the significance of the experience for me; I admit they seem wholly unextraordinary. But the experience itself was fire. It was unclear what part of this lightning bolt stemmed from me and what part from God. In some ways, its intensity convinced me that it could not have emerged from my weak self, which was entirely too fickle and frail for such bold declarations. But in another sense, this conviction seemed to stem from the most authentic part of myself—the spiritual core that knew God intimately, even through veiled vision.

But also, in a strange inexplicable way, the demarcation between me and God seemed irrelevant. In communion with God, we were one and the same—indistinguishable. It was a duet, a dance, a covenant: a gift given and a gift received, a promise made and a promise trusted. It wasn't submission; it was collaboration and union.

After the long wrestle, like Jacob, I had prevailed (Gen. 32:28). Like Sarah, I laughed (Gen. 18:12). I had been given power from God and all was new.

Isaiah had promised that the rivers would not overflow me (Isa. 43:2), and this moment felt like a gasp for air after having been held underwater for too long. It was an awareness of the feathers being lifted ever so slightly—pointing me towards the enveloping air that was present the whole time, embracing me in grace. ⁞•

Over the next few months, my physical health improved and became more manageable. Though it continues to challenge me, and I still have bad days and months, the spiritual epiphany continues to center me when I feel the waters gathering blackness. When I pass through the waters, I remember: the Lord will be with me. And when I flounder in the gap between my hope and my experience, where it's too dark to see, I wrestle.

There's a critique of simplistic religious thinking called "The God of the Gaps." Miracles, so the argument goes, are no longer miracles once we recognize they were accomplished by predictable scientific means—once the unknown becomes known. Was God's creation of the universe a miracle? No, it was the Big Bang. Are answers to prayer miraculous? No, they were coincidence, or medical intervention. That's all.

As our scientific understanding increases, the curtain gradually parts and the mysterious gap where God exists becomes

---

⁞• Because of this experience, Joseph Smith's multiple and differing accounts of his Sacred Grove experience don't particularly bother me. A "crooked, broken, scattered, and imperfect language," according to Joseph Smith, is inadequate for capturing some events, especially spiritual ones.[6] Annie Dillard's description of the struggle was more graphic: "You are a Seminole alligator wrestler. Half naked, with your two bare hands, you hold and fight a sentence's head while its tail tries to knock you over."[7] In my wrestle to find words for this experience, I think I have at least four or five versions by now. I'm revising and rewriting based on new thoughts and new meanings that emerge over time. The alligator wrestle is real.

increasingly smaller. And eventually, once we learn it all, He'll extinguish all together.

No mystery, no God.

But my experience has laid bare a different "God of the Gaps"— not one who exists in the mysterious gaps between knowns, but in the gaps between seemingly contradictory and incompatible truths: God is attentive and worthy of my trust, and God is nowhere to be found. I see this God in the paradoxes, the space where the wrestle occurs. As the thoughtful Latter-day Saint thinker Francine Bennion noted, opposing scripture illuminates some of these gaps:

"Happy is the man that findeth wisdom."
(Prov. 3:13)
"In much wisdom is much grief."
(Eccles. 1:18)

"I will never leave thee, nor forsake thee."
(Heb. 13:5)
"My God, my God, why hast thou forsaken me?"
(Ps. 22:1)

"Men are, that they might have joy."
(2 Ne. 2:25)
"Man is born unto trouble, as the sparks fly upward."
(Job 5:7)[8]

There are no easy answers. The ending of this chapter, in fact, sat unwritten for months. Everything is unsatisfactory. Like an open wound, the gap between the split edges pulses in pain. And though the particulars of each story differ from person to person, we all carry wounds.

In pondering the problem of theodicy, the only place I can go that makes a modicum of sense is that God promises to find us in the gap, to suffer there with us and shepherd us through the muck to make some kind of redemption possible. I haven't found a satisfactory answer to the question of where God is in the muck of life or in the tarantula hawk wasp nests.

When I'm sitting in the dark, the promises make no sense.

But if I instead ask, "What is God doing with me in the muck?," I might have somewhere to go. It helps me to think of God in terms of relationship rather than as a separate entity, a response rather than an existence, a verb rather than a noun. "Christ's atonement," writes Francine Bennion,

> makes it possible for us to go through the meeting of reality, the falling, the hungering, the screaming, the crawling on the floor, the being disfigured and scarred for life psychologically or physically, and still survive and transcend it.[9]

For my part, chronic illness has been a significant catalyst in my search for God. I found myself stuck in the gap between daily weariness and contradictory promises that those who wait upon the Lord shall "mount up with wings as eagles; they shall run, and not be weary; and they shall walk, and not faint" (Isa. 40:31).

There's an unexpected "collateral beauty" in chronic illness. Psychologist Robert Shuman writes that we might "imagine illness as a text, a medium, a way. It is material with which one can work rather than simply an unwanted force to which one is subject. . . . Like the grit in the oyster, the matter of illness becomes the substance of art."[10]

The medium with which those who suffer with chronic illness must build our lives is not the same as that given to the energetic, hospitable Marthas of the world (Luke 10:40–42). But it's a different specialty, a different cell, a different clay, and the result can also be beautiful in the body of Christ. It's the articulate young woman with Down syndrome advocating for special needs rights. It's my grandma with trembling hands, who for years sent shaky, personal birthday cards to each of her descendants. It's my father-in-law, diagnosed with terminal cancer, who would chat with the cashier at the grocery store about the loveliness of the day.

My own illness slows me down, challenging me to pay more attention to the life that speeds by. It turns me toward wonderful books and ideas and conversations, and it invites me to cherish important relationships and not spend too much time nursing my hurts. It teaches me to be patient with others who also have some thorn in the flesh, some challenge with which they wrestle. Chronic illness teaches me about wrestling. And it reveals grace.

Granted, some days I forget all this; there's just fog and weight. At those times I'm drowning in the muck, and the abstract ideal loses footing in the face of the particular reality.

But the same godly tumbling of time and space that brought hawk wasps also brought penguins and wild horses. In the wrestle, new life emerges from death: pain brings perspective and empathy, oranges grow from baked earth, crocuses emerge from ice-encrusted snow, and a phoenix rises from the ashes.

Wounds birth scars.

And I take a breath.

CHAPTER NINE

Playing

What if we've figured God all wrong? We die and hesitantly head up the cloud escalator with a pit in our stomachs. We expect to greet the keeper of points, the tallier of wrongs, the rule giver and taskmaster of the sky. All solemn and serious. Loving, sure, but in the way of a gray-suited, sallow-faced elderly relative who is glad you came but was also slightly disappointed you haven't brought cake.

What if the whole tone was different? Upbeat. A hearty clap on the back and a bear hug. What if He told you a joke? What if the expected He was a She—a Mother in Heaven when you thought you'd be meeting a Father? And what if She laughed with you—one of those minutes-long belly laughs where you can hardly breathe and you snort a little, and when you try to talk it comes out in high-pitched squeaks and tears ooze out of the corners of your eyes?

The God who weeps must also be the God who laughs, or what kind of heaven would it be?

I imagine that when you got to heaven, you'd run around the gardens picking flowers that sported colors you'd never seen before. And there'd be music—not just peaceful harp playing, but also jazz, and dare we suppose, something entirely new? Because surely there'd have been some collaboration for over a decade now between Ella Fitzgerald, Johnny Cash, Johann Sebastian Bach, a Peruvian pan flute player, and an African djembe star.

Likely there'd be a party waiting, a *quinceañera* of sorts where you were the tiara-wearing guest of honor, thrown by God and all your past relatives and friends. Like the prodigal son, you'd be welcomed with a ring for your hand, shoes for your feet, and a fatted calf (though maybe the fatted calf would be vegetarian because do you eat meat in heaven?). You'd get to dive into the misty clouds, do a little teleporting and flying—yes, flying for sure! It would all be a breath of rainforest-fresh air, and you'd feel more awake and alive than you'd ever felt before.

Does this all feel a bit absurd? Blasphemous? Perhaps.

But the prodigal son returning to his father *did* return to a party, not a somber evaluation. And there are far more New Testament references to the kingdom of God as a feast, a wedding, or a party than there are to a courtroom or judgment. How did we miss that? If we envision God with one range of emotion, one way of being, our relationship is limited. In exploring the idea of God, playing with mystery and the unknown, we find space to expand our relationship. These imaginative, creative roamings seem to constitute a kind of theology.

Some approaches to religion feel more doctrinally grounded, telling us the tenets, creeds, boundaries, and limits of our faith. There's an important place for coloring inside the lines this way. By excluding what our faith is not, having clear doctrine helps us understand what it is.

In contrast, an imaginative theology opens us to the possibilities—it's exploratory rather than defined. It takes the unknown of our faith and imagines what it might look like. My attempt, anyway, involves playing with ideas rather than nailing down definitions. And while there is a place for scripts and clearly lit covenant paths, this theology points to something more like open-ended canvases and covenant gardens, just waiting for our imaginative creativity.

In the context of science, the astronomer Carl Sagan once asked,

> How is it that hardly any major religion has looked at science and concluded, "This is better than we thought! The Universe is much bigger than our prophets said, grander, more subtle, more elegant. God must be even greater than we dreamed"? Instead they say, "No, no, no! My god is a little god, and I want him to stay that way."[1]

Sagan was on to something. When I look at science, culture, other perspectives, and other life experiences, alongside my own, I conclude that God must be big. God creates, is surprised, weeps, laughs, and has found endless ways to love. God meets us in houses of worship, in dark alleys, universities, prisons, mountains, hospitals, offices, and playgrounds. We shrink God when we insist on never coloring outside the lines. In the words of the genie in Disney's *Aladdin*: "Phenomenal cosmic powers! . . . itty bitty living space."[2]

In expanding our view of God, we can remember that Jesus said we should become like little children. I don't think this is just because children are often humble, teachable, and forgiving—though of course, those are critical attributes. They also play; they engage with the world without an agenda. Rather than fixating on the past or planning for the future, they interact with the present just as it is. They show us a form of mindful grace that's creative, open-ended, and free.

Adults tend to have an end in mind—wash the dishes in order to have clean dishes to eat from the next day, instead of stretching the warm sudsy bubbles between your palms. Rake leaves to clear the lawn, instead of flinging leaves into the air to watch the bright yellow somersaulting in the sun. Get dressed in the morning because that is the socially acceptable thing to do, instead of dressing up with your fluffy tutu, alligator socks, and superhero cape because why on earth would you not?

Imagine a pot. Adults learn to put the pot on the stove, add some broth, vegetables, beans, and spices, then bring it all to a boil. They let it simmer to make a hearty soup. It's useful and nourishing. It's a very good use for a pot.

Now put that same pot into the hands of a three-year-old. Doing some open-ended exploratory play, suddenly the cooking utensil transforms into a knight's helmet to defend against a fire-breathing dragon. Or it becomes a drum—the wooden spoon sending a *tink, tink, tink* throughout the house. Or the pot could be a bowl, used to collect dried leaves, potato bugs, dandelion heads, milkweed stems, and rocks from the backyard. Turned upside down, it could be a table for a Mr. Potato Head and Superman tea party. Or a stool for reaching high shelves. It could be a marble swirler, a Play-Doh flattener, a boat in the tub, a stuffed-bunny hiding place, a yelling echo chamber, or a frame for a rudimentary rubber band guitar.

There are so many possibilities!

Hans-Georg Gadamer, a German philosopher, studied the philosophy of play. And because he frequently used dense words like *ontology* and *hermeneutic,* I'll pull from the *Reader's Digest* version of Gadamer by yet another philosopher. In a nutshell, play for Gadamer is something in which one is "drawn away from oneself into something beyond oneself." It's a medium in which we get caught up. I imagine it like the flow of a river or a current of air. Gadamer sees play as "effortless, without strain, and spontaneous, always enticing one into more play."[3]

Likewise, the theologian Brendan McInerny has also explored play, which he defines as "those acts that are ends in themselves" and "have no strict purpose."[4]

My son tells me it's just things that are fun—*come on, Mom.*

As McInerny explains, play is totally different from purposeful acts. "Imagine the toddler running around her home, growling and roaring like a lion. To ask what the child's purpose is as she runs around roaring like a lion is almost absurd. Her purpose is precisely to run around roaring like a lion. Her means are identical to her end."[5]

Running around roaring like a lion, drumming the pot with a spoon—this is grace. Freedom. Spontaneity. Creativity. The bird in flight. Engaging in the delight of play—one of God's good gifts. This type of play is powered by grace.

Jesus wants us to become more childlike while also becoming more Godlike. That's a tall order, as it initially seems one path would take us in the opposite direction from the other: one growing down and one growing up. But playfulness may be a way to experience both simultaneously. A *childlike,* open-ended, creative playfulness could be very compatible with evolution, which we could simply see as *Godlike,* open-ended, creative playfulness.

The idea of evolution often feels threatening to people of faith. But evolution as a type of play seems very compatible with faith. Think of it. In the deep past, three or four billion years ago, there was a microscopic life form. God could have used it for some purpose—whether that was for making more little microbes or using it to convert one form of energy into another. It would have been very responsible, professional, and goal driven.

But the material God was using—DNA and its related forms— was malleable, like Play-Doh. It wasn't perfectly reproducible from generation to generation. As the physician and essayist Lewis Thomas put it, "The capacity to blunder slightly is the real marvel of DNA. Without this special attribute, we would still be anaerobic bacteria and there would be no music."[6]

This attribute of life, wherein DNA is subject to change and can therefore express itself in near-infinite forms, is quite compatible with the idea of play. You start with a tiny microbe, and it can become so many forms—redwood trees, kangaroos, bumblebees, tigers, tarantula hawk wasps, great white sharks, yeast, mountain goats, and squid.

But wait a minute; McInerny said that play involves acts that are not strictly purposeful. Even if God set the evolutionary process in motion, didn't He have an end goal in mind, the creation of humans in His image? What about the whole Plan of Salvation and the bringing to pass of the "immortality and eternal life of man" (Moses 1:39)?

Although these are worthy goals, if that's all that we see God doing, we may be looking through too small a lens. Our God may be too small. What about all God's other splendid creations? All the rising and falling tides of dinosaurs and trilobites across earth's history? All the busy microorganisms exchanging goods and services within just one square inch of garden soil? Or the vast expanse of cosmic landscape beyond our own planet's borders? The flaw in this narrow, human-focused thinking is revealed by a sentient jellyfish in Daniel Quinn's Ishmael:

> "For many millions of centuries, the life of the world was merely microorganisms floating helplessly in a chemical broth," began the jellyfish. "But little by little, more complex forms appeared: single-celled creatures, slimes, algae, polyps, and so on. But finally," the creature said, turning quite pink with pride as he came to the climax of his story, "but finally *jellyfish* appeared!"[7]

The story is amusing, and a little preposterous. But it points out that any creature, including humans, may incorrectly view themselves as the sole purpose or final end product of creation. But why would we shrink God to this limited role? All the billions of years of prologue to produce humans, along with all the billions of nonhuman organisms, and then stop the evolutionary flow once the creatures who look like us appear?

Evolutionary biologists sometimes talk about evolution as being non-teleological, meaning not purpose driven. It's open-ended. The possibilities are vast, though they are constrained to a certain degree. We can't have elephants, for example, that get all their energy through photosynthesis, because the surface area of the elephant that can harness the sun's energy is too small to provide enough energy for the large mass of the elephant. To a certain degree, an organism's form constrains how it can evolve. But within those limits, there are still vast possibilities for its expression.

While God is often understood as knowing the end from the beginning and preplanning each minute detail, I would not be surprised if it all looked a little more rambunctious. I think God may have set creation in motion and then played with all the unrealized possibilities.

Our Heavenly Parents may be more childlike than we give them credit for—pulling interesting new forms from old forms, creating lungs from gills, and essentially enjoying the good, true, and beautiful in all their play. Engaging in play as a "bubbly, effervescent form of holiness"—to repurpose a quote from Anne Lamott[8]—I can imagine God being charmed and captivated by the squishy, hairless little humans that made their debut, who then began to take their first steps.

Sign me up for an eternal life of play!

And since this current life is part of eternity, play is equally relevant now. One evening, for example, I sat with my teenage son at the kitchen table. A basket filled with shells served as a treasure trove of fidget toys. My son pulled out two shells.

"Which one do you most relate to?" he asked.

One was smooth, creamy peach—like the old-fashioned orange creamsicles from the ice cream truck. The other was striated, roughly textured, and solid. I chose the ice cream shell, because of how it fit snugly in my palm.

"Hmm," he responded, like he was giving me a psychological evaluation using Rorschach inkblot tests and had just discovered something profound about me. He pulled out two more.

"Which of these do you most relate to?"

There were two turtles made of cowrie shells, glued together with painted-on eyes and wire-rimmed glasses. One of the turtles had a green, woven basket hat, and they'd both been in my collection since childhood.

"I'd say this one," I said, pointing to the one with the hat. "He looks like he's chillin'."

My teenager pulled out other pieces—gray coral that resembled a brain, a polished silver-streaked rock, and a broken piece of conch. He showed me a swirling shell whose inside tunnels were revealed by broken windows on its surface. We listened to the ocean inside it.

Our game basically made no sense and had no rules, but it was easy and lighthearted. We laughed. There was no tension and no expectations. Neither of us had an agenda. It was simply an immersion in flow. Nowhere to be and nothing to accomplish. Simple enjoyment in being present with each other.

It was a small, blessed moment of playful grace.

God's creations may be just as much a result of His play as they are His work. And because we are the result, God's play is reflected in us. Gerard Manley Hopkins's beautiful poem illuminates this idea.

> As kingfishers catch fire, dragonflies draw flame;
> As tumbled over rim in roundy wells
> Stones ring; like each tucked string tells, each hung bell's
> Bow swung finds tongue to fling out broad its name;
> Each mortal thing does one thing and the same:
> Deals out that being indoors each one dwells;
> Selves—goes itself; myself it speaks and spells,
> Crying What I do is me: for that I came.
>
> I say more: the just man justices;
> Keeps grace: that keeps all his goings graces;
> Acts in God's eye what in God's eye he is—
> Christ—for Christ plays in ten thousand places,
> Lovely in limbs, and lovely in eyes not his
> To the Father through the features of men's faces.

The just man behaves justly—he "justices." The grace he bears is revealed in all his daily activities. He "graces." He's gracing.

> Acts in God's eye what in God's eye he is—
> Christ—for Christ plays in ten thousand places.

The man of justice and grace behaves how God sees him; God sees him as a manifestation of Christ, who is everywhere.

> Lovely in limbs, and lovely in eyes not his
> To the Father through the features of men's faces.[9]

Man's pure being is a manifestation of Christ's presence within him, a conglomerate of human and divine. Man's whole being—bound up with Christ's presence—is beautiful to the Father.

Just as birds and dragonflies are filling the measure of their creation by sparkling with iridescence in the sun's light, and just as stones and strings and bells are simply themselves by making the sounds of stones and strings and bells, human beings are who they are when they are themselves. And we are most ourselves when Christ is at play in us—when we show justice, embody grace, and manifest Christ through our actions and faces.

Christ plays in ten thousand places, through all of creation.

We live in Christ when He lives in us—not for mere efficiency and usefulness. We are bright, delightful, and beautiful simply when Christ is at play in us. He may also be at work in us, of course, but there's an important nuance. It's the difference between toil and delight. Sure, He's doing something with us, as in the parable C. S. Lewis famously quoted from the theologian George MacDonald where we are a house, and God is knocking down walls and adding wings, and it hurts.[10] But He's also alive in us, right here, right now, lighting up our lovely limbs and eyes.

Playing in grace, we are a bird.

"Great Scott, what have we here?!" God exclaims. In delight, God marvels at a mockingbird in freefall, an albatross soaring across oceans, a flash of kingfisher, a hummingbird suspended in midair, a scarlet macaw blazing red across the sky.

A girl who can't breathe for laughing.

And here we are, enthusiastically drumming on our pot. Calling out our name.

The world is joyfully and exactly as it should be.

CHAPTER TEN

Resting

Every twenty-four hours or so, around ten or eleven at night, I forget who I am.

On a typical evening, I scrunch up my pillow just minutes before oblivion, turn onto my right side with my knees tucked toward my chest, and push my body backwards into Michael's open arms. The memories of the day and the plans for the morning settle like dust. My breathing deepens and slows, my jaw slackens, and all my muscles melt. The room fades along with my consciousness. And then I am gone.

Sleep is a strange diversion. We spend a whole third of our lives doing it, lost in an unresponsive, passive state of being when we could be eating, working, playing, or reproducing. And it's not unique to humans. As far as we know, almost every animal species engages in some version or other of sleep—becoming unconscious of their needy babies, unaware of approaching tigers, and oblivious to the vital food supplies around them. From an evolutionary perspective, to have a characteristic be so ubiquitous yet lead to such astounding vulnerability, we'd conclude that sleep must be critically important for survival, or we'd have disposed of it long ago.

Even animals for whom sleep seems particularly catastrophic have figured out ways to adapt. Dolphins, for instance, need to surface every few minutes of every day and night for a breath of air so they don't drown. That's as potentially disruptive and inconvenient as needing a sip of water every few minutes throughout the night. But instead of eliminating sleep, dolphins have evolved a way to allow just half of their brains to sleep. Dolphins can literally be half-asleep. After a period of time, the other hemisphere takes a turn so that the whole brain can be refreshed.

Birds, too, have evolved remarkable adaptations. Migratory birds, which travel thousands of miles across oceans, have learned to indulge in brief, seconds-long power naps while in flight. Other birds, when congregating in groups, have been known to align themselves in a long row along the ground. Most of the birds will be completely asleep, but the bird on the left will keep its left eye open and its right hemisphere awake, while the bird on the right will keep its right eye open and its left hemisphere awake. As a whole, the flock then has a view of approaching threats without completely eliminating its shuteye.

It turns out that all these acrobatics to preserve sleep seem to be worth the effort. Along with nutrition and exercise, sleep is increasingly touted as one of the three essential foundations of health. There's much we still don't know about the benefits of sleep, but it appears to benefit almost every aspect of the body.

For one, sleep is like a nightly cleanse. All the busyness and activity of the day causes a buildup of toxins, proteins, and memories in the brain—much like how my kitchen table looks after someone's creativity has dreamed up a project using soap, toothpicks, and googly eyes. Sleep clears out the excess and discards unnecessary memories while filing away important ones. Sleep is an archivist.

Sleep also resets our emotions. This is probably why my husband and I decided early in our marriage that the traditional advice to never go to bed angry did not work well for us; a good night's sleep tempers emotions so that conversations are easier. Sleep helps us approach the challenging situations of the day with some emotional steadiness. Sleep is a therapist.

Creativity is also enhanced by sleep. During the dreaming portion of sleep, our brains forge connections between relatively unrelated areas, bypassing the well-worn neurological pathways in favor of the roads less traveled. My brain may pull a memory of eating black licorice with Grandma and Grandpa, combine that with the anxiety of being told I have bad breath, and weave that into trying to find my child's teacher to give her a stuffed bear on teacher appreciation day. This hodgepodge of emotions and thoughts seems to have implications for enhancing creativity—pulling together disparate ideas to form new ones. Sleep is an explorer and a teacher.

Beyond these benefits, sleep also enhances our capacity to learn, memorize, and use rational thought. It strengthens our immune system and our ability to fight cancer and infection. Sleep is a bona fide superpower.

All this inner work occurs without our direction and input, when something other than our conscious will is effecting change. It all takes place when we *stop* trying. We simply turn off and let go.[1]

In addition to waking and sleeping, life is rhythms: working and resting, uphill and downhill, inhaling and exhaling, contracting and relaxing. It's tempting to see the downhills simply as the recharge—as if we were a cell phone plugged into the wall at night, merely gearing up for the tasks ahead. But I believe there's more to it than that.

Turning off allows other mechanisms to work in us than what we'd initiate from our very useful but sometimes stubborn, self-concerned, and imperceptive brains. There's much that can be "accomplished" while detaching and emptying. In Annie Dillard's words, "Experiencing the presence purely is being emptied and hollow; you catch grace as a man fills his cup under a waterfall."[2]

It can be tempting to see this kind of rest as laziness or inefficiency. And it's true that within the Church much good is accomplished through service and busyness. But if we forget to inhale, it can quickly lead to burnout and a sense of meaningless nothings. Our work can feel hollow when the sound of our running feet drowns out the still, small voice that guides our steps.

Meditation as rest is one area I have been exploring. One form is contemplative prayer, which was foundational for early Christian saints. In many strains of Christianity, including within the Latter-day Saint faith, this practice has largely been forgotten. But those who recognize its value are increasingly reviving it and sharing it across boundaries of faith traditions.

The contrast between contemplative prayer and my own prayer practice reveals that the speaking part of my prayer often feels like a gallop: *Thank-you-for-this-day.*

Please-bless-the-food-that-it-will-nourish-and-strengthen-our-bodies. Please-bless-us-to-get-home-safely. It's lots of petitions, lots of to-dos, and lots of hurry.

Contemplative prayer instead feels like the inhaling breath that precedes each exhale—the listening to the speaking of prayer. Thomas Keating, a Trappist monk and prolific writer, teaches that when Jesus reminds us to go to our closets to pray, He is inviting us into that inner room of the contemplative heart where we commune with God. In prayer, thoughts will appear unbidden, our agendas and plans pulling us away from this sanctuary. Our busy brains have jobs to do. But these intrusions, he says, are like boats floating down a river.

Notice them, Keating invites. Let them float by. Then gently return. Consent to God's presence and His work within you. Much like sleep, something happens when we're in this restful state, apart from any work we initiate. Our only effort is simply a decision to participate.

As I understand it, the practice involves being completely receptive and embracing an intention to be open and present to human-divine relationship—a restful existence in communion. We stand with our empty cup ready to be filled. Rest in be-ing rather than do-ing. "Centering prayer," writes Keating,

> is a way of awakening to the reality in which we are immersed. We rarely think of the air we breathe, yet it is in us and around us all the time. In similar fashion, the presence of God penetrates us, is all around us, is always embracing us. Our awareness, unfortunately, is not awake to that dimension of reality.[3]

The South African Archbishop Desmond Tutu once said, "I am learning to shut up more in the presence of God." As opposed to a "shopping list" prayer, the Archbishop said he was "trying to grow in just being there. Like when you sit in front of a fire in winter, you are just there in front of the fire, and you don't have to be smart or anything. The fire warms you."[4]

Spiritual and secular resources abound to teach these practices. Various forms of stillness, relaxation, calmness, meditation, contemplation, and mindfulness have emerged from both the East and West. In taking baby steps, I notice gracing marked by a stillness that spills out into my daily activities in unexpected ways.

Once, for example, in the middle of a busy day, I was practicing a violin piece to perform at church. It was a beautiful number: "Savior, Redeemer of my Soul." Alongside inspiring lyrics and talented musicians, I wanted to prepare well. But it was not an easy violin part. The notes approached dog-whistle pitch—very high with numerous ledger lines past the standard treble staff. And sometimes it felt like a Hail Mary pass to launch my finger up the string and land on the correct note.

As I concentrated and drilled, at one point I noticed a tension in my hand and shoulders. In what felt instinctive due to my meditation practice, the observation of tension initiated an easing in my shoulders and a softening of my fingering hand. My bowing arm relaxed—still firm but in a way which allowed the bow to glide smoothly rather than rigidly against the strings. The tone of the notes became clearer and more resonant. The quality of the music shifted ever so slightly. It was subtle, almost imperceptible.

The moment of noticing the tension and the subsequent relaxing felt so familiar and so much like meditation that I am sure the one must have influenced the other. The substance and practice of rest improved my work, though I could not have anticipated that occurring with the violin. I wondered how many other unexpected places this quality might manifest.

Another time, and in a more critical area, Michael and I had been feeling stuck with one of our teenagers. Resolving the prevalent tension was foremost on our minds. Our son was irritated and confrontational and expressed frustration that we didn't support him. There's a book series called *How to Hug a Porcupine*; though I hadn't read it, the title was an apt description of where we found ourselves.[5]

In one tense and heated moment, I remembered that in this space we never seemed to resolve much. One of us needed a breather, a little stillness perhaps. Probably me. In a moment of quiet and pause, I realized that maybe we needed more time, more reflection, in our interactions.

What if I texted him?

After a time, I sent the first text—an olive branch of sorts. I acknowledged his frustration and explained how I would like to know how I could better meet his needs. There was a pause, and then a long text came back.

It was vulnerable.

Honest.

He could say things through a screen that he hadn't been able to say in person. He was uncertain, showing me the ways he was in pain. The format of the conversation allowed for slowness and reflection.

I listened, thanked him, and related where I could. The conversation ended, leaving one of my questions hanging. The quality of the conversation, like the quality of my violin practice, felt softer—calmer and less driven.

At the time I thought that not much was resolved, but the next day was just pleasant. It was like the heat had been turned down in all our interactions. He smiled, asked for advice, and just seemed more comfortable in his own skin. He seemed like himself. In standing down and relaxing our porcupine quills, we'd found the ease of God present in stillness.

This subtle quality of rest is also illuminated by the Sabbath. God created the world in six days and saw that it was good, and on the seventh day He rested. God blessed the day and made it holy. God's children are commanded to hallow the Sabbath day— meaning to make it holy, to consecrate or sanctify it. We are to set it apart for rest.

Other than for the purpose of an occasional nap, I hadn't thought much of the Sabbath as a day of rest. When I was a child, there were things we did differently on Sunday—we didn't go shopping or play with friends, for example. Instead, we went to church, and we often had a roast dinner.

Unlike other families, my parents didn't emphasize listening only to church music or viewing only church movies, because shouldn't your media be good every day of the week? Sometimes we wrote in our journals or read scriptures together—but not watered-down children's versions, because my parents believed in the power of actual scriptures, even for young children. And sometimes we did homework on Sundays, because learning is also good any day of the week.

As an adult, my Sabbaths are largely like how they were as a child—though we try to avoid homework, we play hymns in the morning, and we're more likely to have burritos instead of roast. But with busy church callings, get-togethers, and responsibilities, I haven't quite understood what rest has to do with the day.

I'd like to learn more from the Jewish conception of Sabbath. The rabbi Abraham Joshua Heschel writes of the Sabbath not simply as a day *without* something, but *with* something. Toil is replaced with an almost tangible holiness. The Sabbath, he writes, "is a day for the sake of life. Man is not a beast of burden, and the Sabbath is not for the purpose of enhancing the efficiency of his work. . . . It is not an interlude but the climax of living."[6] In other words, it's not a means to an end but an end in itself.

Other religions have *places* of holiness—temples, cathedrals, and mosques. But Heschel says that for the Jews who were scattered and without a home for so long, holiness was created with cathedrals of *time.* This set-apart time has an aura of holiness. He writes,

> Unless one learns how to relish the taste of Sabbath while still in this world, unless one is initiated in the appreciation of eternal life, one will be unable to enjoy the taste of eternity in the world to come. Sad is the lot of him who arrives inexperienced and when led to heaven has no power to perceive the beauty of the Sabbath.[7]

It's as if Heschel learned to welcome the restful paradise of heaven into an earthly day and to see the Sabbath as a harbinger of eternity. His daughter, Susannah Heschel, writes of the preparations, joyful anticipation, lighting of the candles and welcoming of the sunset on Friday evening. She describes the following day as featuring prayer chants, services, challah bread and chicken soup, walks, reading, naps, conversations, and a general atmosphere of sanctity. For her, the day was transformative.[8]

Reading both Heschels' words, I can sense that the two have cultivated a relationship with the day, as if they're spending it with a cherished friend. It's not simply a day to abstain, or tune out, or get through, but a day to relish. And it's not simply a rest *from* labor, but a rest *in* God. It's a day that nourishes and sustains, whose very climate is distinct from other days, when "the air of the day surrounds us like spring which spreads over the land without our aid or notice."[9]

The whole picture feels to me like an insightful vision for how my own Sabbath worship could grow. Shifting my focus could turn a day that simply passes by into an experience of grace. Rituals could guide me to meaningful experiences.

"Ritual" used to seem like a bad word. It's the thing you do because that's what you've been told to do; it's devoid of anything substantial; it's vain repetitions that obscure rather than reveal God. No plucking corn on the Sabbath; limit your steps; don't pick up your bed to walk. And truly, rituals can be hollow.

But as Heschel illuminates, rituals practiced with intention can point us toward holiness, a deeper relationship with divinity, and rest. So much depends on our orientation towards the practice—and whether the ritual has become bland or nourishing through repetition.

My sons run cross-country, and their running has a ritualistic rhythm: it occurs in both the morning and the afternoon, in sun, rain, or snow, from January through December. But a couple times a year, they participate in "active rest." They cross-train. While remaining physically active through alternate exercise like biking or swimming, they strengthen muscles other than those commonly used in running. It's a way of allowing certain muscle groups to rest, preventing injury from the constant pounding of feet on pavement.

The rest of sleep, meditation, and Sabbaths can also be a kind of cross-training. We humans are good at getting ourselves stuck—of grinding into our well-worn paths, doing things the way we've always done them, maximizing efficiency, and racing from one thing to another. In doing so, we strengthen some muscles but neglect others. Incorporating rest can be a meaningful shift.

My road took a turn when the COVID-19 pandemic hit, and I was relieved from my Sunday School teaching calling for a time. Activity yielded to rest. In the solitude and disconnect from my usual responsibilities, I turned to writing about the gospel instead of teaching it. Social, scheduled learning yielded to personal, self-motivated learning. And that's when the writing for this book began. In resting one set of muscles, I was able to strengthen another. Cross-training allowed the well-worn paths to give way to new forms of grace.

We may learn that life becomes both more enjoyable and more successful when we learn to take a break under a shade tree, turning from our white-knuckled clinging to the iron rod toward a more restorative, gentle orientation. As in the science of sleep, so much inner work takes place when we let go. Like the bird in flight, transformations can occur when we stop trying so hard, shift our focus, and embrace what is present.

Stillness can be woven into my day. I can ease into a conversation, quiet my chattering mind during my commute, or take a moment to breathe the sunshine streaming through my front window.

Emptying myself, I have room in my cup for a waterfall.

CHAPTER ELEVEN

Storytelling

There's a story many of us have heard: Once upon a time, we were born broken—sinful and degenerate. There was a chasm separating us from perfection. From our first breath, we fell from grace. Adam's sin was stamped on us from the beginning. Our only hope was Jesus, who would impute His righteousness to us, snatching us from the inevitable trajectory of our own corrupt natures.

It's the story of Original Sin. Though officially we Latter-day Saints reject the story, in practice we keep returning to it. We retell it with a twist. We agree it's not Adam's fault, but we affirm that it is ours:

We're still not good enough, and God will keep punishing us and letting us suffer until we are. He sends trials to purify and perfect us. Jesus will eventually wrangle us into starched shirts and straight pews, but it will require a lot of work on our part. We must put our back into it, and maybe—just maybe we'll reach the heavenly destination.

The story needs a revision. A truer telling. Something like this: Once upon a time, we were born whole—magnificent and holy. As literal children of God, we were fashioned with the spark of divinity. Perfect and pure. As we grew, at times we forgot that we were "trailing clouds of glory," as William Wordsworth wrote,[1] and we rejected the gift of grace because we were convinced that we could do it on our own. In our suffering, we forgot both who we were and whose we were. We built up walls to separate us from God and each other. But Jesus intervened, sitting with us until we remembered—and sharing His life with us once we did.

The philosopher Adam Miller tells a version of this story that he calls Original Grace, and he juxtaposes it against the story of Original Sin. This version begins with grace, not sin. Miller writes, "My goal in life is not to prove that I will eventually deserve some future grace or salvation that God is currently withholding. Rather, my single Christian obligation is to stop rejecting the grace and redemption that God is already and continually willing into being."[2] Wherever we are right now, at our core, we are bathed in grace. Once we discover this, we discover ourselves and simultaneously discover God. You could call this process healing, repentance, or gracing. It's all the same story.

Indulge me for a moment in a fish tale. Once upon a time, long before duck-billed platypuses or dinosaurs, a funny-looking fish was born. His pectoral fins were not sleek and aerodynamic like those of his brothers and sisters. They were stout and awkward, like beefy stumps jutting from his sides. Though he tried to keep up with his friends, he was often picked last for games and was the butt of all the jokes.

Mama told him he was special—that the stars and moon shone extra bright the night he was born. She called him her little slice of heaven; she'd take his face in her fins, her penetrating gaze reaching deep into his soul, and tell him he was magnificent. But he didn't understand what she meant, and he retreated to the shadows.

The venerated church elders took Mama aside to speculate as to why God would give her dear child this trial. Perhaps Mama had forgotten to say her prayers. Maybe she harbored an unholy pride and this was her penance.

Or maybe the boy was to blame. Maybe he had sinned before he came to the ocean—he was a fence-sitter or a half-hearted, less-than-valiant milquetoast soldier, and this was the penalty. Maybe repentance was the antidote. Or perhaps, the elders speculated, there was no cure and the boy had been sent to teach everyone patience and compassion.

Mama listened, but she quietly rejected the idea of a God who would punish her beautiful boy. Deep down, she knew God was love. Both her heart and head told her that God was not vindictive or punitive. And she knew her boy was more than an object lesson; her little slice of heaven was magnificent.

The fish physician, weighed down by age, wisdom, and spectacles, took Mama aside. Perhaps, he suggested, he could design some prosthetics to facilitate easier movement through the water—amputate the aberrant fins and design some artificial ones that could attach to and be controlled by her son's nervous system. (Technology was shockingly quite advanced.)

Before Mama had a chance to respond, an up-and-coming fish genetic engineer who had overheard the conversation broke in. Perhaps, the engineer suggested, she could sequence the boy's DNA and locate the anomalous pattern. She could repair the mutant DNA in some of the boy's select stem cells, allowing the mended cells the opportunity to grow new fish-appropriate fins. (Indeed, medical technology was tremendously cutting edge.)

At this point, the church elders, physician, and genetic engineer all began to quarrel about the best way to put the boy into their fish-shaped mold—to build the template and cookie cutter to get this boy to rights. They pulled out their graphs and scriptures, their white boards, arguments, and data.

Meanwhile, from the corner of her eye, Mama saw her boy venturing toward the edge of the world where the water, sky, and land all converged. It was dusk, and the quarreling faded into the background.

Mama swam to her son and then stopped, catching her breath. In awe, she watched as her boy dug his strong fins into the sand, propelling himself forward. She surfaced just in time to see him pull himself onto the land. His unique-looking fins, the object of ridicule and speculation, were now a superpower. All along, he had been a fish with legs. A whole new world awaited, ready for exploration. The stars and moon shone extra bright. He looked back at Mama and smiled.

They knew. He was magnificent.

In our own stories, we often lack Mama's vision. In both ourselves and others, we focus on the pieces that don't "fit." We seek explanations for what we label as imperfections, and we are quick to judge difference as inadequacy. We don't have the recklessly optimistic view from a mother's eyes. We're blind to the glory.

Once on the coast of Vieques, one of the small islands off Puerto Rico's main island, I saw the glory that others before me had not. A winding bus ride took me and my family to Mosquito Bay, where we were told that at night, bright bioluminescence lit up the ocean. When the bay's water is disturbed, billions of microscopic creatures called dinoflagellates glow in the dark. They light up like fireflies.

After the sun went down, we ventured out in kayaks. We put our oars into the dark bay, and the water surrounding them glowed a blue-green neon, as if illuminated by halos. The kayaks in front of us sat on soft iridescent cushions of water. Cupping our hands to scoop out handfuls of ocean, we saw that the water sparkled with glitter. And when we poured the water onto our thighs, it danced like sparklers. It was magic.

Our tour guide for the evening told us that the natives—the Taíno (TI-no) people—used to say this bay was the place that stars were born. The stars in the black sky and the fledgling stars in the bay seemed like the stuff of poetry.

The colonists, on the other hand, upon seeing this unusual bay, described it as devilish and evil. They blocked the river feeding the bay in hopes of destroying it. Ironically, their efforts did just the opposite, increasing the bay's rich soup and hence the dinoflagellates' growth. Ever since, through hurricanes and varying degrees of human activity, the bay has waxed and waned in how brightly it glows. It is currently one of the brightest in the world.

Both the Taínos and the colonists noticed the bay's peculiarity. But the colonists rejected it while the natives embraced it.

The Indigenous people didn't try to explain or fix the anomaly; they sat in awe of it. Like Mama fish, they saw the magnificence.

Being like Mama fish or the Indigenous people reminds me of Father Gregory Boyle, who has worked for over twenty years with recovering gang members in Los Angeles. He and his associates run Homeboy Industries, which provides everything from job training to tattoo removal to a place of love for those who often feel discarded and rejected. In his beautiful book, *Tattoos on the Heart,* Boyle reiterates over and over that the process of healing for these young men and women involves not a fixing of what's wrong with them, but a discovery of what's right. Redemption looks more like an unveiling than an overhaul.

One of Boyle's "homies," Willy, a confidence man with an outsized bravado, weaves together his Spanish and English in a moment of searing clarity. He drops the tough-guy posturing and simply says, "God . . . thinks . . . I'm . . . *firme.*"

"To the homies," Boyle explains, "*firme* means, 'could not be one bit better.'" The news is a revelation. It replaces the story of the "one false move" God with an experience of the "no matter whatness" of God. It replaces Original Sin with Original Grace.[3]

Boyle is convinced that these rough, outwardly broken outcasts are the light of the world as Jesus taught. Boyle points out what Jesus does not say, which is that *"One day, if you are more perfect and try really hard, you'll be light.'* [Jesus] doesn't say *'If you play by the rules, cross your T's and dot your I's, then maybe you'll become light.'* No. He says, straight out, 'You are light.' It is the truth of who you are, waiting only for you to discover it."[4]

My husband's mother, who works with young children, many with autism and other special needs, speaks in a similar way. Each child, at their core, is good—even the outwardly misbehaving and attention-starved ones. They are not problems in need of correction, but goodness in need of discovery.

She tells me of a beautiful boy with big brown eyes. He's often volatile, and teachers have scratches and even bite marks to prove it. He also has a piercing gaze that pleads to be seen—to be known. Who he is at his core is not the same as the mask he uses to conceal himself. Deep down, he knows this. My mother-in-law knows this. She shines with conviction when she explains.

As a mother, I also want my children to know this by heart. If I had a redo, this would be my daily bedtime story: You are *firme*. You are light. You are bioluminescence and glory. Soak that up. Write it on your heart.

I see this but forget it, and I often fail to communicate it. On one difficult day, my young son was angry and let it be known. The specifics evade me now, but it's likely there was yelling, throwing, a clenched jaw, and a face streaked red with tears. I was exasperated, with shallow breath and a gut in knots. Probably I yelled, because, for the love, child!

Finally, my little boy wore himself out and collapsed on the bed. He curled up against the wall like a letter *C*, as if willing himself to be as far away from his family and this day as possible. A dim night-light illuminated his sleep and cast shadows on the wall. He hadn't bothered to change clothes or get under his covers. His angry little body had finally settled into slow breaths.

Watching him sleep, my own body relaxed, and love for this small tyrant overcame me. I just wanted to hold and comfort him, but I knew he wouldn't have had it.

I stealthily lay down next to him on the narrow twin bed, like I used to do when he was a toddler. Minimizing any mattress movement that might disturb him, I curved my body inches from his while still leaving space. I lay there and willed light for him—breathed love for him. He needed something he didn't know how to find and I didn't know how to give. So I prayed without words for him.

I knew he was good. Wholly magnificent. In all the ways he hadn't yet figured that out, I knew. His passion was an asset, as were his strength and independence. In love, that much was clear. My breathing slowed to match his. My body relaxed beside this powerful little boy. He was clothed in God's grace; he always had been. Even in the dark, I could see.

There's a universal truth we recognize in this, and it emerges in our cultural stories. Consider Darth Vader, the quintessential bad guy, from the original Star Wars trilogy. He was king of evil and callous destruction. Yet his son, Luke Skywalker, felt there was still good in him. There was still light. In the end, Darth Vader's redemption came through Luke, who helped him rediscover his own light. That's how he was saved.

The scriptures are always inviting us to see holiness in unexpected places. We're told to stop worrying about the circumcised and uncircumcised, the Jew and Gentile; forget about the clean and unclean, the saved and unsaved. Jesus was constantly being asked questions about who deserved the prize and who didn't: Who is my neighbor (Luke 10:29)? Did that blind man sin, or was it his parents (John 9:2)? What must I do to receive eternal life (Luke 10:25)?

But Jesus rarely gave straightforward answers, which may point to the wrongness of the questions. In gracing, we don't question who our neighbor is, but instead respond to our neighbor. When confronted with blindness, we don't ask who sinned, but anticipate and facilitate God's compassionate response. We don't calculate precisely what we need to do for eternal life, as if computing the minimum effort to get a passing grade, but simply realize that with Jesus, we already have it. We already shine with God's presence. We're already chosen.

At the end of earth's story, we teach that the lion and the lamb will lie down together (Isa. 11:6)—the carnivore and herbivore, the unclean and the clean. The familiarity of the image obscures how provocatively it upends our expectations. I like to think this means that in the end, there will be no more wrongheaded divisions into holy and unholy. We'll all shine. We'll all lie down together.

It's not a matter of finally getting everyone sorted into heaven and hell, but in simply seeing each other and ourselves. With clear-eyed honesty, we break down the walls that hide us from each other. We pull off the dark masks that shield us. The grand story is not a perfection of all of us into God-shaped molds, but instead a collective smashing of all the molds. Without our faulty judgments and divisions, we can finally see the face of the God-imbued beings before us: "For now we see through a glass, darkly; but then face to face: now I know in part; but then shall I know even as also I am known" (1 Cor. 13:12).

So here, then, is how the story goes. It's short and sweet. We are born, cradled by grace. We live, illuminated by grace. We sin, rejecting grace. We suffer, blind to grace. We heal, succored by grace. We love, empowered by grace. And we die, embraced by grace.

Look out the window. Do you see it?

Look in the mirror. Does it shine?

Returning

I've heard it said that the foundational problem for Western religion is sin, while the problem for Eastern religion is *suffering.* I wonder if these two problems are more closely linked than we realize, since both fundamentally involve what feels like an acute separation from God. In both cases, we may be far from home and unaware of how to return. We find ourselves outside the flow of grace.

There's a fascinating TED talk by the journalist Kathryn Schulz called "On Being Wrong," which has implications for what it's like outside the flow of grace. In this talk, Schulz poses the question, "What does it feel like to be wrong?" The audience gives a few answers: embarrassing, thumbs down, dreadful. Schulz then suggests that the audience has been answering a different question: ing a different question:

what it feels like to *recognize* we are wrong. She suggests that being wrong, before the moment we recognize it, doesn't feel like any of these things. Instead, it feels like being right.[1]

Granted, many people are actually right when they think they are right. But tellingly, the most egregious sinners also often think they are right. The Pharisees during Jesus' time obeyed all the prescribed steps religiously. Tyrants brought "order" to chaotic societies. Mass murderers brought "righteous retribution" on those who bullied or ostracized them. The more benign sinners among us are not immune to this either. We justify our mistreatment of others because we were hungry or because *they* did it first. We find internal self-justifications and perform mental gymnastics to convince ourselves that we are in the right. We have deep core vulnerabilities—needs for esteem, control, power, and safety—and sometimes we act out in harmful ways while telling ourselves elaborate stories about why our behavior was justified. These acrobatics result in what has been called our *false self.*

There are different iterations of this concept, with slight nuances between them. There is the *false self* or the *shadow self.* The Latter-day Saint philosopher Terry Warner describes it as *living a lie.* Each describes how for various reasons, we hide the truth about ourselves from ourselves. In Warner's book, *Bonds That Make Us Free,* he tells an illuminating story that shows how we do this. It's relayed by a thirty-something-year-old businessman named Marty, who says,

> "The other night about 2:00 A.M. I awoke to hear the
> baby crying. At that moment I had a fleeting feeling,
> a feeling that if I got up quickly I might be able

to see what was wrong before Carolyn would be awakened. It was a feeling that this was something I really ought to do. But I didn't get up to check on the baby."

Warner explains that Marty's first impulse to help his wife had been an honorable one, calling it his felt moral imperative. Initially, Marty knew in his heart that getting up was the right thing to do. But when he didn't follow through, Marty had to come up with reasons to excuse himself so that he wouldn't have to admit to being a scoundrel. This is what he came up with:

"It bugged me that Carolyn wasn't waking up. I kept thinking it was her job to take care of the baby. She has her work and I have mine, and mine is hard. It starts early in the morning. She can sleep in. On top of that, I never know how to handle the baby anyway. I wondered if Carolyn was lying there waiting for me to get up. Why did I have to feel so guilty that I couldn't sleep? The only thing I wanted was to get to work fresh enough to do a good job. What was so selfish about that?"

The question of whether or not Marty's reasons were fair is beside the point. If he had been really exhausted, he could have simply asked his wife to take a turn with the baby. The point here is that in order to justify his behavior, Marty found it necessary to accuse his wife. He was victim, judge and jury, and by playing all these roles he exonerated himself while convicting his wife.[2]

This case building is required in order to hide the complicit part of ourselves from our awareness. That deep, hidden side divides us from our true selves. It separates us from the flow of grace. So how, then, can we return?

I think we can learn something from a Christmas cactus that sits above my kitchen sink. The plant was given to me by my husband's mother. She has a gift with plants and can coax beauty out of even the most persnickety varieties. The Christmas cactus, thankfully, is quite forgiving—convenient because my not-so-green thumb is often in need of forgiveness.

Around Christmas each year, the plant explodes in a spray of flowers that roughly resemble hummingbirds—some red, some pink, as if the plant can't quite pin down its favorite color. The leaves are thick, no doubt designed for water conservation, with spiked edges, and are linked in chains like a toddler's pop-together beads.

These leaves, like other plants, exhibit phototropism wherein they turn their faces toward the light. The cells in the stems that are farthest from the light elongate in response to hormones, thus propelling those nearest to the light to move even closer. The cells also strategically rearrange their chloroplasts—the suncatchers of the cell. Like little domesticates, the chloroplasts harvest and bottle sunshine for future energy use. I can sympathize with their need for sun, especially during the cold of Christmas.

Every now and then, I turn my plant 180 degrees and watch over the next couple days as the leaves, slightly disoriented, gradually reorient themselves toward the light. Unlike radical butterfly transformations, this one is soft. Like a newborn rooting for her mother's breast, it's a subtle yearning, the slowest of stretching, the most understated movement.

This movement reminds me of *repentance,* which comes from the Greek *metanoia,* meaning a change of heart and mind—a conversion, a healing, a turning, a spiritual overhaul. The word *repentance* unfortunately carries with it a lot of baggage such as penance, shame, and the idea that heaven must be earned, so the word is a mixed bag. But the reality it points to is worth noticing.

Gracing, I believe, is this reality. Repentance is the journey of turning to God again and again. We forget to join with God, and then we remember. We think we are right, and then we realize we are wrong. We stop living a lie. We stop telling ourselves stories that keep us stuck. We live with ego-driven, narrow vision, and then, as with a camera lens, we zoom out and see that God was present all along. Our experience and story changes. God offers alternate views, relationships, healings, and ways of being and seeing—over and over.

But through a softer lens, we also heal from our accumulated wounds. With Jesus, people who are blind see. People who are deaf hear. People who are lost are found. The lines between sin and suffering blur, but the solutions continually return us to grace. With Jesus, we wake to a new story and to the reality of a world embedded in grace. Of recognizing,

> *Oh, this person is my brother.*
> *Oh, God was always here.*
> *Oh, this hope is bigger than my pain.*
> *Oh, there are colors and light and beauty I didn't*
>   *see while living a solitary, detached life.*

Every time we return and are transformed, we are saved. Every time we forget, we are damned—literally stuck, because there is no salvation without God.

We are saved by grace. Full stop. This is no cheap grace—a mere saving proclamation that we need Jesus regardless of any work we do. Rather, we are saved by grace because the freely given gift envelops us like air and does what it was designed to do.

Grace saves; work doesn't. Work does other things. Knives cut and soap cleans. Work gets things done and displays God's love. And grace saves.

Living without God, on the other hand, is the state of what the Book of Mormon calls "the natural man." I don't mean natural as in earthy and without makeup or artificial dyes, but as in "without God," as Alma teaches (Alma 41:11). This supposedly "natural" condition is a false front that we put on, wherein we are an enemy to God simply because we have placed ourselves apart from God, in opposition, and not on the same team. This way of being is faulty, guarded with plates of armor. It's not how we were designed to function, and it's contrary to the nature of God and the nature of who we are. We weren't created to flourish as a branch dismembered from its root.

In life, we tend to toggle between these different ways of being—with God and without. Far from God, we become stuck in suffering and sin. Returning home, we re-enter God's embrace.

Reminiscent of my Christmas cactus, a similarly subtle movement once happened between me and my brother. Prior to this, dysfunction had plagued me and my siblings for various reasons—contention and hurt between various members that had occasionally turned into painfully ugly confrontations. People had been flat-out rotten to each other.

My family of six siblings and parents all live within an hour of me, so we have traditionally held family dinners to connect. Because of all the tension, though, I'd been hesitant to host.

One brother's personal life had been brutal, including a painful divorce and ongoing court battles. He understandably felt like much of his life was out of his control and was therefore extremely sensitive to others exerting control over him. His strong political views were also highly alert to any element of control. We'd had disagreements on that topic. And his fuse seemed short.

In finally making the leap to host dinner, I wanted to minimize the potential for conflict. So, I added structure to the event. Rather than our typical pattern of eating followed by unstructured play and conversation, I planned a show-and-tell where all the cousins and adults could participate. I planned to show my Johnny Apple peeler that cores, peels, and cuts apples into long, curly, slices. I emailed the invitation to my family. My brother responded with his intention to share "what's really going on in the world"—not-so-subtle code for his contentious politics.

Oh boy. So, then I sent a clarifying email about the structure of show-and-tell—a limited amount of time so everyone could have a turn, with the event structured more as a presentation than a discussion. I also requested that if anyone wanted to have a confrontational or argumentative conversation with anyone else in the family, that they please take it away from the group.

My brother responded that he wouldn't be coming—that I was censoring and controlling. He essentially argued that my approach would deepen divides. In suppressing free speech, I would be putting up barriers to future resolutions. I was allowing underlying issues to fester, ignoring deeply rooted problems, and putting on a façade of fake niceness. In retrospect, I see that his concern was like Martin Luther King, Jr.'s concept of *negative* peace in which there was an absence of tension in place of *positive* peace in which there was the presence of understanding.[3]

At this point, I buckled down with renewed intensity, engaging in one hundred-plus back-and-forth emails with my brother and other family members. I was blown away, but not entirely surprised, that my request to take confrontation elsewhere was deemed so objectionable. At one point, I used an analogy that I hoped would connect with my music-composing brother.

Music, I said, needs both structure and flexibility. The structure includes a certain key signature, time signature, and other conventions. But if the music becomes too structured, it lacks room to breathe, becoming flat and boring. There needs to be balance. In creating an event, I said, too much flexibility leads to mayhem while too much structure stifles spontaneous expression. For the family dinner, I was leaning toward more structure; he wanted more flexibility.

Finally, we compromised and agreed that debates or disagreements with civility, respect, and good faith were okay, but contentious arguments that indulged hostility or contempt would have to be moved elsewhere. No topics would be off-limits, and my brother reasserted that he'd share his controversial topic for show-and-tell.

Sunday evening came. I was apprehensive. But when my brother came over, something in the air had changed. We hugged, and I noticed a black paperback about the composer Johann Sebastian Bach in his hand. My brother might be Bach's biggest fan, and in my family, no one disputes Bach's greatness. I don't know what happened between our email exchange and the event, but for show-and-tell my brother completely dropped his plan and instead shared a story about Bach once taking a random melody given to him by the King of Prussia and turning it into an interesting piece of music with various opposing yet complementary lines of harmony. My brother demonstrated on the piano.

At the end of a pleasant evening, right before my brother left, I explained how because I had been a violinist, I was used to playing the melody. I didn't have a good sense of how chords worked together in the interplay of melody and harmony, but I had great respect for composers who did.

"Would you like me to show you some basics?" he asked.

"Yes," I said.

He sat on the piano bench, and I sat with him. He showed me the structure for the easiest key: the tonic chord, up a fifth to the dominant chord, and down a fifth to the subdominant chord.

"These are your basic chords," he explained, and with that structure in place he demonstrated moving up and down the keyboard, introducing novelties and flexibility, and always remembering and returning to the tonic chord—your home.

So, there we were. Two middle-aged adults, old enough that we were both going gray, sitting on a piano bench. Just me and my big brother.

He taught me how to combine structure and flexibility to create harmony. Mostly I saw flying fingers in a lot of different places, and I couldn't quite keep track. But there was a pinprick of clarity in the chaos. I was figuring it out. Maybe there's hope for us both.

Looking back, I see how we were butting heads. I can remember the frustrated, for-the-love-of-all-that-is-holy energy in my chest. We were without God—isolated, hurting, and in our natural state. We had both known we were right, and maybe we both were to some degree. I'm not even certain if our interactions had been due to suffering or sin, but the distinction may have been irrelevant. We were Christmas cacti with our faces toward the dark.

But openness to God returned us to each other for an evening. In love, we stopped weighing our responses and simply made room in our hearts for each other. Grace taught us to respond with what was needed rather than what was deserved. We communicated in ways that allowed us to drop our self-protective armor and be open to each other. The relationship transformed into an open, giving, substantive, and meaningful harmony. As far as I'm concerned, in that moment, we were saved.

Within cultural Christianity, we may have largely misconstrued the whole business of being saved. *Repent and be saved. Accept Jesus and be saved.* But that kind of saving always seems to refer to some distant time down some distant road—after death, after judgment, after perfection, after now. It's the donut for the end of Family Home Evening, the trophy for a job well done.

I think Jesus wants us to be saved now. "Wake up, sleeper, rise from the dead, and Christ will shine on you" (Eph. 5:14, NIV). The Doctrine and Covenants teaches that "there are many kingdoms; . . . there is no space in the which there is no kingdom," and that we will only enjoy that which we "are willing to receive" (D&C 88:32, 37).

Is it really so different now?

We live each day with what we are willing to receive. Become a new creature, we are taught. Let the old person die and the new one rise. Let the self-pitying, stuck, tunnel-visioned, closed, asleep, unseeing, unhearing creature die, and become the lit-up, awake, open, healed, present, gracing creature who is alive in Christ.

Ironically, my brother with strong political views is frequently telling me to wake up. There is great evil in the world, he says, and we need to be on guard against its insidious manifestations. I don't doubt he's right about that, and through our conversations I'm learning to better recognize corruption that hijacks government and corporate systems, misdirecting them to serve power and money rather than people.

Also, though, there is great goodness in the world. We'd do well to wake up to that too. When alive to grace, we learn how to better respond to evil and pain, both in others and in ourselves, with the goodness that is available and needed.

There is power in grace—not the twisted, self-serving, authoritarian kind of power, but the inventive, collaborative, compassionate kind. When we jointly tap into that well of goodness while simultaneously stripping off the natural man or woman, we radically transform the world. And for each person who wakes up, we come one step closer to Zion.

Together, we reach for light.

The journey returns us home.

CHAPTER THIRTEEN

Perceiving

A scene in the cult fan favorite *Monty Python and the Holy Grail* depicts an illness-stricken village in which collectors of the dead pull a cart through the street. "Bring out your dead!" they call. One old man, carried from a house and about to be discarded on the cart of bodies, protests, "I'm not dead!" There's some annoyance about such technicalities, and after a brief argument, the collector knocks the old man unconscious and the poor soul is thrown onto the pile of corpses.[1]

This could well be a scene playing out in the lab of Harvard University's E. O. Wilson, nicknamed the "ant man" for his leading role in the field of myrmecology—ant biology. Ants,

Wilson noted, are incredibly attuned to the chemicals in their environments. In contrast to humans, who perceive their world largely through auditory and visual channels, ants *see* and *hear* chemicals—they *smell* and *taste* their way through the world. An ant's world is awash in chemicals that function as warnings, maps to food and mates, and rallying battle cries. An ant's data collection mode is thus radically different from our own.

This is apparent in how they treat their dead. Sometimes, after an ant dies, she lies there in the middle of the colony, legs crumpled, while her sisters simply ignore her—walking around her and going about their business as usual. But after a couple of days, the ants suddenly notice their deceased friend, pick her up, and dump her into the garbage heap. What triggers this sudden awareness?

Wilson hypothesized that a specific chemical marker might be what alerted the ants to the existence of their dead comrades. After experimenting with various chemicals smelling of locker room, body odor, garbage dump, rotting fish, and sewer, he eventually narrowed it down to a chemical called oleic acid. (His poor lab assistants!) Wilson tested his hypothesis by creating a living corpse—daubing a tiny bit of oleic acid onto a living ant and then watching how her friends would respond. Sure enough, the surrounding ants converged onto her, picked her up, and dumped her into the ant cemetery. I imagine the not-actually-dead ant wriggling and yelling, "I'm not dead!" But her friends couldn't hear her. She smelled dead, after all.[2]

This is just one example among many in the vast animal world illustrating what the Baltic German zoologist Jacob von Uexküll called an *umwelt* (OOM-velt)—essentially a unique sensory world as it's perceived by a particular creature. All the inhabitants of our world are embedded in a shared environment which teems with sights, sounds, vibrations, chemicals, and fields of magnetism and electricity. But each species is only attuned to some of these aspects—its own narrow sliver of reality, its own unique sensory bubble, its umwelt.

Humans, for example, are not able to see ultraviolet light like bumblebees, feel the air currents created by passing flies like spiders, smell all the myriad flavors their pet dogs can, or track the magnetic fields of the earth like loggerhead turtles. But they can visibly perceive ants that don't look dead. Humans are aware of colors and sounds that are hidden to other animals, such as patterns on animals' bodies that those very animals are unable to see, or decibels produced by animals that those very animals cannot hear.

But we shouldn't assume that humans are the special ones. Low frequency infrasonic sound waves like those produced by earthquakes are silent to us but can be heard by animals such as elephants and whales, while our ears are completely oblivious to the high frequency ultrasonic sound waves produced by bat and dolphin echolocation, dog whistles, and motion detectors. What is darkness to us is color for some; what is stillness to us is vibration for others. Each umwelt both illuminates and conceals a portion of reality.[3]

It seems we are drastically constrained. It's an easy mistake to assume our umwelt is all there is because that is all we know. But understanding this bias points to overwhelming truths that exist just beyond our perceptual awareness. What realities are as glaringly obvious to other creatures as a wriggling ant would be to us? What realities exist outside the umwelts of most, if not all, of earth's creatures? Do we grieve our dead, for example, not because they are gone, but because they have simply slipped beyond our perceptual awareness—the color we can no longer see, the sound we can no longer hear?

God is presumably not constrained in this way. As the one who encompasses all the umwelts—the ultimate perceiver—God is aware of each falling sparrow and every tear on every face. Within God's perception, I imagine, is an igneous rock which has roiled in the tectonic shifting of plates and has begun to disintegrate again into magma. God perceives a single atom of iron that has just incorporated itself into the hemoglobin of my neighbor's pet leopard gecko.

I imagine God is not only aware of these things by sight, as I have pictured them in my head, but by their sounds, colors, and temperatures. God knows these things by their smells, electrical fields, gravitational pulls, and magnetic pushes. In the case of that iron atom, perhaps God is aware that it tastes like a paperclip; it emits atomic vibrational whispers; it exerts the tiniest gravitational pull felt on the opposite side of the universe. In all its perceptual forms, God is aware of the first kiss, the tree falling in the forest, the new star's birth, and the spiritual rebirth. God perceives the aha moment, the unnamed angst, and each pulsing, blooming creature.

This all seems overwhelming and frankly chaotic—a trillion billion sounds, thoughts, colors, pains, and creatures, just for starters. What a cacophony! If in any given moment you were acutely aware of everything from the microbes setting up shop on your eyelashes to the breathing of a mole rat on the opposite side of the planet, how would you function?

According to Aristotle, the force behind each of these perceptions, presumably God, stands apart, beautiful and perfected.

God is the unmoved mover—the one who has both foreseen the mole rat and put him there. God causes all movements while remaining Himself unmoved. God orchestrates all, perceives all, and remains unchanged in the process. The Episcopal priest Barbara Brown Taylor characterizes this God as a "very old white-bearded man on a throne, who [stands] above creation and occasionally [stirs] it with a stick."[4]

But there's another way to view God. The Jewish philosopher and theologian Abraham Joshua Heschel turns the ancient Greek concept around and explores God as not the unmoved mover but the "most moved mover." Heschel teaches that the biblical God is characterized not by His perfection but by His concern for the world. The idea of the aloof, ideal God is replaced with one who is embedded with us here and now. Aware of all, God is moved by all. God does not merely answer our prayer from atop His mighty throne, but "shares our prayer" in the middle of our mighty mess. God weeps with us, laughs with us, is invested in us, and draws on us; Heschel provocatively claims that not only are humans in search of God, but that God is in search of us. He writes that *covenant* is a "mutual bond embracing God and man, a relationship to which God, not only man, is committed."[5] It's a collaborative reaching.

As I imagine it, the covenant God is immersed in a vast sea vibrating with billions of heartbeats. God remains aware of each as if through peripheral vision—supremely alert and in search of intimacy. Suddenly God focuses in on one heartbeat. Previously hardened through years of suffering and sin, this heart has briefly let down its guard, softening in response to a kind memory. God perceives this reaching and reaches back. The intimacy moves both the heart and God, and they now beat in unison. In response to this grace, now both God and the heart seek other like-minded reachers, and both continue the work of moving and being moved.

Barbara Brown Taylor imagines the most-moved-mover God as part of an "infinite web of relationship, flung across the vastness of space like a luminous net." Far from static and aloof, this God "is all over the place. God is up there, down here, inside my skin and out. God is the web, the energy, the space, the light—not captured in them, as if any of those concepts were more real than what unites them—but revealed in that singular, vast net of relationship that animates everything that is."[6] A moved mover needs to be aware of all that is present. In the middle of the cacophony, God could then say . . . there! And there! Inspire this heart, move this creature, light up this darkness. God does not stay still.

We humans, on the other hand, lack God's agile maneuverability in part because our perceptual awareness is more constrained. Some portions of reality are, in this life at least, concealed. We have a species-specific umwelt. And to hijack the biological concept still further, there are also intraspecies biological, cultural, and environmental umwelts existing among distinctly different humans.

I perceive the world with an astigmatism, both literally and figuratively. I'm a North American, five-foot-six, adequately fed, English-speaking, stay-at-home suburbanite who was raised LDS in a middle-class home. These parts of my perception will always constrain what portion of the whole I can perceive. But I don't need to resign myself to complacency; by simply recognizing my limitations while also learning from people who perceive the world differently, my limited umwelt can expand. I can approach my neighbors with a kind of holy curiosity.

Take Jewish writers, for example, who often perceive *law* more generously than many Christians; with their unique vision they rcdccm the term. Law in its various forms—commandments, ordinances, rituals, and the like—transforms from rote routines and checklists to meaningful practices and duets. "The law, stiff with formality, is a *cry for creativity*," writes Heschel, "a call for nobility concealed in the form of commandments. It is not designed to be a yoke, a curb, a strait jacket for human action. . . . All observance is training in the art of love."[7] If my only picture of law is from the rigid hands of the specific group of Pharisees in Jesus's time, I'll miss the expansive Jewish thinking that also sees love as the heart of law. Before Christians existed, the Jews taught, "Love your neighbor as yourself" (Lev. 19:18). And like Paul, the great advocate for grace, Jews explained that the purpose of law is for it to become written inwardly on our hearts, not merely for it to stagnate on tablets of stone (Jer. 31:33).

In Jason Olson's memoir, cowritten with James Goldberg, Olson writes of holding both his Jewish and Latter-day Saint faith. He explains that "being a Jew meant hearing the beat of a divine drummer. The law, so often viewed with derision by Christians, brought a divine calibration to our people. It brought a sense of sacred order syncing our calendar and daily life with God's heartbeat."[8] The law, then, is one way to attune ourselves to God's heartbeat—to hear decibels outside our own umwelt.

Indigenous people often perceive other truths; they reveal the heartbeat of the earth. "When I close my eyes and wait for my heartbeat to match the drum," writes Robin Wall Kimmerer, "I envision people recognizing, for perhaps the first time, the dazzling gifts of the world. . . . Blankets of moss, robes of feathers, baskets of corn, and vials of healing herbs. Silver salmon, agate beaches, sand dunes. Thunderbolts and snowdrifts, cords of wood and herds of elk. Tulips. Potatoes. Luna moths and snow geese. And berries."[9]

I imagine astute Indigenous hearers such as Kimmerer with a stethoscope against the earth, seas, and sky, listening to the verses of song created by not just humans, but the rest of the living world. Creation teems with music. To view our connection with God as detached from our plant and animal cousins is to miss the family reunion. As I learn more of what Indigenous people see from their vantage point, I approach my own life differently. Breaking through the sunbaked crust of my garden with a trowel, watching the fleeing ants and wriggling worms, I'm grateful. Paying attention, I squeeze a Concord grape from its slippery, purple peel, smell the ripened cherry tomato on the vine, and taste the sun-ripened sweetness of both in my mouth.

The heartbeat of the earth is then joined by another. Contemplatives from all religious backgrounds amplify the heartbeat of silence. What I once assumed was a retreat from the needs of the world is instead an immersion into a better understanding of it—into a different sort of air. Listening more closely, I feel the vibrations of my body when it is settled rather than frenzied, and I experience a breath that is cleansing, deep, centered, and large. The Sufi mystic Rumi wrote, "I have oft laid the ear of my soul at the window of the heart. I have heard much discourse, but I have seen no lips."[10] Paying attention, the silence in my heart speaks, and I hear the low, slow, deep tones—like whale songs.

These tones are joined by those who hear the heartbeat of justice. Often regardless of religious affiliation, these hearers occupy an umwelt wherein they respond to a call to repair broken and unjust systems. They refuse to perpetuate poverty, neglect the needy, imprison the innocent, gut the earth, and marginalize the other. In their critique of harmful behavior and systems, these hearers are unwilling to throw God under the bus because "God said so" or because "Jesus will come again and repair it." They engage with suffering and, like Martin Luther King, Jr., perceive love as "the heartbeat of the moral cosmos."[11] Their love calls them to display injustice front and center so it can no longer be unheard. Paying attention, my umwelt expands further.

Immersed in the cacophony of all these sounds, this is what happens for me today. I sit here writing, and my dog walks up to me, her brown eyes imploring. She's new to our home. Coincidentally, her name is Izzy, just like our previous dog who had died. We found Izzy Two in the classified ads—a seven-year-old mountain cur who hunted mountain lions and bears in her prime. After she was injured once too often, her owner sought a comfortable home where she could live out her days.

Gently, Izzy's warm breath calls me back, and I pat the short-haired bristle of her caramel head as she arches upward, stretching the skin of her neck taut.

Sitting in this place, listening closely, I remember that the law tells me that the "righteous care for the needs of their animals" (Prov. 12:10, NIV); Indigenous teachings invite me to see Izzy not just as my property but also my cousin; contemplative teachings call attention to the way her nervous energy settles when I touch her, and also how mine does the same; and the heartbeat of the moral cosmos teaches me to care for the least of these. So, I take a short break, and we go for a walk.

This may be how God responds to the cacophony. Participating in reality with us, God perceives all and then responds in customized, creative ways. And as children of God, we can follow suit. Sometimes we are moved to bring all our compassion and intelligence in responding to a grieving friend; or to direct our ingenuity to address a work problem or right a wrong; or to glean from scripture, family history stories, and past interactions answers to our children's questions. The more we have diligently gathered and the more expansive the borders of our umwelts, the more we have to offer. The more responsive we are to being moved, the more capable movers we become: "Neither take ye thought beforehand what ye shall say; but treasure up in your minds continually the words of life, and it shall be given you in the very hour that portion that shall be meted unto every man" (D&C 84:85).

Jesus was a moved mover with the words of life at his disposal. Once, amid chaos—a throng of people pressing and crowding in on him—he showed what that meant. I imagine the narrow street—everyone pushing and shoving, people with their wares and animals en route to and from the marketplace, people trying to get to Jesus or someplace else. Jesus was also on his way to somewhere critically important: Jairus's twelve-year-old daughter was on the verge of death, desperately in need of care.

Yet despite that important errand and amid all the competition for his attention, Jesus perceived a touch on the hem of his garment. He described it as virtue, or power, going out of him. I picture it in the outermost periphery of his awareness, possibly as subtle as an air current created by a passing fly. But it was enough. Jesus could return all else to the blurry background and shift focus to the most needful thing: one imploring woman who had been hemorrhaging for twelve years. He reached her faithful reaching and responded: "Daughter, be of good comfort: thy faith hath made thee whole; go in peace" (Luke 8:43–48).

Wholeness is created in this covenant, reciprocal reaching. Watchful and agile, God has the entirety of creation in view. And then God's attention shifts to one focus, one person. In response to God's reaching, a single individual joins with God—becoming whole, connected, and transformed. This object of God's care, sustained by God, then reaches others. Those who, like God, are moved movers, who are connected and perceptive, become instruments in God's hands. Eventually, through patience and an abundance of grace, we are made whole.

I visualize this movement from cacophony to wholeness by way of a unique population of fireflies. The phenomenon these lightning bugs exhibit has something to do with math—chaos theory, specifically, and how unpredictability acquires order. Also, though, I think it has something to do with theology.

Along the humid banks of a mangrove forest in Thailand, the fireflies wait. Dusk deepens, and a spontaneous flash lights up the leaf litter. A second later, a few feet away, another. Then another.

At first, the flashes seem disconnected and random. But gradually, as the fireflies become more aware of their neighbors, their sense of rhythm syncs. Two spontaneous flashes in the foliage occur simultaneously, then four. The small groups coalesce in the increasing nightfall. Eventually, as if led by a conductor's baton, the whole forest pulses in tandem like a festive Christmas light show. The disparate internal and external beats merge. A web of isolated individuals joins together in a synchronous energy. In response to the light of others, each firefly becomes both moved and mover.

In gracing, our expanding perceptions reach beyond the umwelts that constrain us. Light moves us and we reply by displaying our light to others. Eventually, we tune in to the harmonious heartbeat of God and all creation. We see the light. Our increasing sense of interconnectedness calls us to expand our own slice of reality to perceive and incorporate, as much as possible, our neighbors' umwelts.

We see the invisible and hear the inaudible. The deaf hear, the blind see, and the dead wake. In covenant relationship, we join God in becoming moved movers. Like God, we do not stay still: we inspire this heart, move this creature, light up this darkness.

Oneing

Before this life, when we were waiting in lines to pick up brain microchips, I must have overlooked the line labeled *Sense of Direction.* I should have paid more attention to the Canada geese and salmon patiently waiting there. I won't make that mistake again.

Unlike my husband, Michael, who guides people out of wild mountainous terrain with the county's search and rescue team, I am hopelessly directionally impaired. I'm in awe of people who can orient themselves in unfamiliar places. Or even familiar ones, for that matter—like those who can go into a store at the mall, browse for socks, and then miraculously come out knowing which direction to continue walking. Don't tell, but were it not for heaven-sent Google Maps, I'd get lost driving to most of my family members' homes.

Sometimes I drive through an unfamiliar location and have a vague intimation that I have been there before. My brain is swimming underwater in a murky kelp forest where it's trying to right itself—to orient itself on the map. Trees, houses, and signs enter my field of vision like strangers. I stare at them with a vague *déjà vu,* trying to place them, feeling like we may have met before.

And then all of a sudden it's as if the roads shift into the sky and the houses peel off the pavement. The world generously reorients itself around me, and I know where I am.

I have another intimation: we're embedded in a matrix where the dividing lines between us are more fabricated than real. I look at my hand and remember how I used to trace its outlines to create a Thanksgiving turkey; this five-fingered boundary denotes where I end and the rest of the world begins. I have imagined my spirit in a similar way, like a shadow embedded in reality or a transparent cardboard cutout of my physical form.

It wasn't always this way, though. As newborns, we entered a strangely foreign world filled with unfamiliar sensations. Swaths of light and color. Achings in our gut. Wailing pitches of sound. Every now and then, one of the fleshy swaths of color would appear suddenly into our line of sight and bonk us on the nose. Or we'd experience an unprovoked scratch. Other times, the world breathed softness. Warm milk. Safe and tender touch.

Over time, we realized that the fleshy swath of color was connected to a larger form that we could move and control—it was simply our own arm. If we didn't want our arm to appear out of nowhere and hit us in the face, we effected change. If we wanted the toy keys rattling above our car seat, we reached for them. If we wanted assistance from the responsive beings around us, we appealed to their faces. And when that wailing sound pierced the air, we discovered we could close our mouths and it would disappear.

In order to interact with others and our environment, we had to realize what was us and what was not. Psychologists call this process *individuation.*

The understanding of where we begin and end is useful information. We hold the controls for our own human-shaped forms. Others hold the controls for their human-shaped forms. We are all agents that can act, and we have an environment that can be acted upon.

But this understanding also comes with a cost. That's my impression, at least, gleaned from my own moments and from both science and the teachings of mystics, prophets, and poets. We are all slightly disoriented in an unfamiliar neighborhood, swimming around in the kelp, struggling to remember.

Our vision is veiled, but every now and again the frayed edges of veil flutter and part. We remember that we're embedded in a shared matrix of sensation and interconnection and that we are not entirely our own. The Latter-day Saint scholar and spiritual seeker M. Catherine Thomas has written of individuals who have experienced profound religious experiences, sometimes described as mystical, in which they had "dramatic shifts in awareness." An element that often binds their stories is a recognition that "their own being, which once had felt separate and isolated, was in some way actually at one with all animate and even inanimate things. The ordinary objects of life took on a brilliant sheen for them which filled their souls with joy."[1] They were no longer separate from the rest of creation but fully a part of it, and of God.

Christian thinkers have made similar observations through the centuries. The Christian mystic and theologian Julian of Norwich called this shared connection "oneing." She wrote,

> This beloved soul was preciously knitted to God in its making, by a knot so subtle and so mighty that it is oned in God. In this oneing, it is made endlessly holy. Furthermore, God wants us to know that all the souls which will be saved in heaven without end are knit in this knot, and oned in this oneing, and made holy in this holiness.

Elsewhere, she explained, "The Love of God creates in us such a oneing that when it is truly seen, no person can separate themselves from another."[2] This concept is reminiscent of another word: *Atonement.* At-one-ment.

We've seen how infants need to conceive of their separateness in order to grow and reach their potential. And we've seen that our highest state of being may be that of union with everything else. So which is it? Are we separate or one?

Lacking boundaries between ourselves and others is called "failure to individuate." Psychologically, it can lead to submitting in unhealthy ways to domination and abuse. Those who fail to individuate are forever dependent on others' opinions. They don't have healthy boundaries and fail to develop confidence and autonomy. It's a weakness of my own personality type.

Other people have the opposite problem. They vehemently reinforce their separations with barbed wire and bulletproof glass. They become static and immovable in response to the beings around them. In the words of Simon & Garfunkel, they become a rock. An island. Isolated, unaffected, and alone.

My father-in-law, just a few weeks before he died from colon cancer, shared his perspective on this question as it related to the afterlife. He had long since left the Church, and his journey led him to other spiritual paths. He talked about vibrational energies and manifesting your desires to the universe. The afterlife, he believed, involved entering a kind of shared consciousness. I pictured a background of black space where a small orange cloud, newly emerged from the blue and green earthy sphere, merged with a larger orange cloud.

I see conceptual hints of *oneing* in my father-in-law's description. My hang-up with his description, however, was that it seemed to involve an erasure of self. If I'd asked at the time, maybe he would have elaborated on this and alleviated my concern. I wasn't too fond of the idea of melding into complete uniformity and hence nonexistence. I don't want to disappear. I'd like to retain my personality, unique gifts, consciousness, and even odd quirks, if possible.

Sometimes in religious discourse, we imply that disappearing is the goal. We *submit* to God. We obey. We subjugate our will to God's. In becoming godly, we strip more and more of ourselves away until nothing is left. We become swallowed up in Christ. We turn off our desires, dreams, internal moral compasses, brains, and hearts and become robotic followers. That sounds more like Satan's plan: yes sir, no sir. We vanish.

Upon further thought, I've decided that true oneing cannot be the erasure of self. According to a paraphrase of the ancient Greek bishop Irenaeus, "The glory of God is every creature fully alive."[3] Not gone, not dead. *Alive.* Jesus said that when we lose ourselves, ironically, we also find ourselves. We are more vibrantly ourselves when we are alive with others and with God. Far from erasure of self, oneing may look more like revealing of self—a shedding of all the "natural human" layers that get in the way of our core true selves. Maybe my father-in-law believed this too.

Though it makes little logical sense, I believe we may be simultaneously distinct and one. Jesus demonstrated this possibility by likening himself to a vine and us to its branches. "Abide in me, and I in you," he taught. "As the branch cannot bear fruit of itself, except it abide in the vine; no more can ye, except ye abide in me" (John 15:4).

Fruit borne from a vine reminds me of an apple tree in our backyard. It's a four-in-one wherein each branch produces a different variety of apple: fuji, gala, yellow delicious, or red delicious. Before we purchased the tree, the four branches had been grafted onto a common rootstock. When our dog, Izzy, was in her chewing puppy stage, she got hold of one of the branches, peeling it roughly from the tree. Frustrated, my husband rescued the small branch and placed it in a cup of water to soak. A day or two later, he fitted the jagged edges of the tree and the branch together like a puzzle and then secured it all with duct tape.

After eight or nine years and another chewing attempt by Izzy, the branch, still not much more than a twig, still struggles. It has yet to bear fruit. But it lives. Every year it produces leaves, and one day it will surely be strong enough to support an apple.

Jesus is the apple tree, and He's the vine. We are the branches. Dismembered, we wither and die—a languishing twig on the ground, whose green fragments will fade to brown. But bound up in Christ and receiving nourishment there, we live and produce our own unique variety of leaf and fruit.

That's oneing. It's grace.

Jesus has another example: "Come unto me, all ye that labour and are heavy laden, and I will give you rest. Take my yoke upon you, and learn of me; for I am meek and lowly in heart: and ye shall find rest unto your souls. For my yoke is easy, and my burden is light" (Matt. 11:28–30).

When we roam the grasslands on solitary hills, isolated from Christ, our burdens are heavy. But with a weighty, wooden yoke binding us together at the neck, we become partners. Ironically, the weight is no longer crushing. Two distinct beings, bound by a yoke, we pull together as both separate and one. Like the theological concept of indwelling, wherein the divine presence resides within us, these yoked oxen call to mind one entity instead of two—that as Christ said, "you are in me, and I am in you" (John 14:20, NIV).

The bird in flight is also separate and one. On her own, she flaps and falls and lands on her rump. She's a disconnected branch, no different from the solitary ox. But embraced in grace, she flies. She's gloriously herself and at one with God, with whom she is dancing. She's gracing.

Yet oneing is not solely confined to a relationship between us and God. Grace, I'm coming to believe, involves a oneing between us and other beings as well. As the mystics recognize, we are moved by others, welded to them, interdependent with them. The natural world exemplifies this.

Imagine the bird in flight joining her flock of friends. They are starlings and together form an enchanting murmuration. The individual birds move together in sync as if they are one super-organism, stretching and contracting, leading and following, all without physically touching. It's a mesmerizing, choreographed dance, if you've ever witnessed one. Some scientists attribute this phenomenon not to avian telepathy, but to simple laws of physics—essentially mathematical representations of creation. Each bird seeks to minimize its distance from the flock by adjusting its position relative to the several birds closest to it, while at the same time leaving the maximum amount of space to prevent midair collisions. Thus, the birds are both separate and one.[4]

Social insects, such as bees and ants, behave similarly. Rather than existing as separate beings, performing their separate little tasks, they behave more as individual cells within a single body. They each have their specific jobs whether that be nursing the young, cleaning or repairing the hive, impregnating the queen, or foraging for nectar. It's reminiscent of separate individuals in the whole body of Christ.

The field of ecology, too, shows how each cog in creation's apparatus is inseparably bound up with the others. It's all about relationships and interconnectedness. The sun becomes grass, the grass becomes an ox, the ox dies and becomes dirt, the dirt becomes a tree, the tree creates an apple which I pluck from a duct-taped twig, and the apple then becomes me.

Some up-and-coming companies expedite this interconnectedness by incorporating a deceased person's ashes into a root ball for a tree or bush. I wouldn't mind becoming a lilac one day. Or a peach. But even if I end up in a socially acceptable coffin, I hope the white satin lining isn't the only thing in there with me. I'd like a warm, colorful quilt, because I dislike being cold. And something organic, like roses, because they'd improve the smell down there and provide a little oxygen. Eventually, though, I hope to give up my solitary ways. I'll diffuse my way through the casket wall and concrete vault to fully incorporate with the vibrant web of life again. I'll give back to the same earth that has given so much to me.

Our interconnectedness is on full display in creation, and it was also revealed by Joseph Smith. A prime subject of his theological reflections and teachings had to do with sealings, gatherings, and unity—or in Julian of Norwich's terminology, oneing. "If ye are not one ye are not mine," it says in the Doctrine and Covenants (D&C 38:27).

Jacob Baker, a doctoral student in theology, posits that Joseph Smith's vision was one of "a grand, cosmological redemptive unification of the entire human family, indeed, the entire universe, sealed and welded together in one resplendent chain of Being." Across time and space, on either side of the veil, the work of God is a great "welding together."[5]

As an analogy, welding is an interesting choice. Baker quotes the scholar and author Jared Hickman, who explains that "welding" is a better term than the usual "melting pot." In welding, "individual units are intimately related to each other, bleeding into one another at the point where they are soldered together, even as they retain something of their integrity. Whereas the melting-pot . . . denotes a wholesale homogenization whereby individual units are broken down into a single mass."[6]

Welding, then, is not disappearing into an orange cloud. It's not erasure at all but a fusing of distinct beings through unbreakable bonds—both separate and one. Baker says Joseph Smith was not interested in collapsing the world's diversity into sameness, but in exploring "the expansive possibilities of human relatedness and integration at their most intense and sublime."[7] In other words, not a melting-pot soup but a welded-together work of art.

A major message of the restoration is that it's not enough to cultivate our separate and distinct relationships with God. Our separateness is a mirage; "they without us cannot be made perfect—neither can we without our dead be made perfect" (D&C 128:15). We are in the process of building Zion, and when we inevitably clash and conflict with others, we'd do well to stop hitting ourselves in the face. Doing that makes as much sense as autoimmune disease, where the body turns its arsenal against itself. Other beings are our hands and eyes and knees in this shared body of Christ. For better or for worse, mortality is a group project. If we poison the community well to destroy our neighbor, we are also destroying ourselves.

When we step back, the big picture emerges. Many beings inhabit one living, breathing earth. Astronauts often speak of having an awed sense of global consciousness after viewing our tiny planet from afar. The space shuttle commander Jeff Ashby once explained, "Seeing how fragile the little layer is in which all of humankind exists, you can easily from space see the connection between someone on one side of the planet to someone on the other—and there are no borders evident. So it appears as just this one common layer that we all exist in."[8]

Just one perfect whole. In the Church we talk about Jesus being perfect and about us needing to be perfect. But perfection in the scriptures implies more an idea of wholeness and completeness rather than flawlessness. What if Jesus's perfection lies in the idea that He is in perfect relationship with us? As the Franciscan priest Richard Rohr has said, "God loves things by becoming them."[9] God is incarnate in Jesus and incarnate in us and incarnate in all of creation. Jesus already came and is in all of it—from the "least of these" (Matt. 25:40) to the greatest.

What if our perfection also lies in us becoming whole—not just in terms of our individual selves, but as in no longer separate from any other being?

Maybe we were wrong to think we'd pass through the pearly gates in isolation. When the dark glass through which we now see shatters, it may very well be that our world will generously reorient itself around us. The roads will shift into the sky and the houses peel off the pavement. The vague *déjà vu* will open into a resplendent reality.

We'll wake up and approach the throne of God through the cloudy orange heaven as one family—bound, oned, and welded to each other through grasped hands. As the naturalist and environmental philosopher John Muir noted, "When we try to pick out anything by itself, we find it hitched to everything else in the universe."[10] We enter heaven with our dead not only because we bear responsibility for them, but also because they are hitched to us.

We'll discover that all of us are air, water, and ash. We're flocks of birds, bees, vines, and yokes of oxen. Like Jesus, we'll bear not only the shame of the world, but also its glory. The metal of our sealed hands will merge with the flesh of our separate bodies— the bond and free, the Jew and Gentile, the lamb and the lion.

Oned in God.

All of us.

Collecting

None of the ideas I hold closest are entirely original, though sometimes in my narrow view I want to give something new and original as my mark on the world.

My dad, a professor of philosophy for over forty years, tells me that's not how ideas work anyway. All of us are collectors and curators and puzzle reassemblers. He tells me this is an ancient Hebrew view that sees truth as what arises from the heterogeneous soup of past expressions and not as fixed realities.

Evolutionary processes work similarly; each reproductive cycle pulls from the existing stuff and creates new combinations never before seen. Ideas, like antelopes and lilacs, emerge from existing raw materials rather than appearing magically.

God didn't create *ex nihilo,* out of nothing; He was an organizer, constantly pulling from the stuff of the universe for His creation. Radically, He may not be God in the sense of being supreme architect over all. Rather, He is God because He works within a context of preexisting natural laws and because of His radical faithfulness to what is already there, our own selves included. To paraphrase the Catholic theologian Ilia Delio, our lives are entangled "in the ever-newness of God's creative love."[1]

For art in particular, but with creation more generally, the poet T. S. Eliot likened this creative process to a chemical reaction, that the mind is "a receptacle for seizing and storing up numberless feelings, phrases, [and] images, which remain there until all the particles which can unite to form a new compound are present together."[2] We collect, and then we synthesize. We are social creatures, always pulling from the flowing streams of ideas, cultures, and languages in which we find ourselves.

Ultimately, our creations don't come out of the blue. This book is not *ex nihilo.* I've collected trinkets of truth from books and conversations and presented them here along with my own stories. I've taken care to give credit where it's due, but it's impossible to wholly extricate my own thoughts and language from the seeds that were planted by others. I'm a curator. We all are.

Obviously, the subject of this collection is grace. If you've gotten this far and are still unable to give an all-encompassing yet concise definition of grace, that makes two of us. But defining the *word* was never my intent. I am much more interested in the phenomenon and experience than I am in the definition.

Maybe the following from the scientific realm will clarify what I mean. Biology means the *study of life.* Yet, as supposed experts on the study of life, biologists have found very little agreement on what *life* is.

As the science writer Carl Zimmer explains, definitions range from "Life is the process of existence of open non-equilibrium complete systems that are composed of carbon-based polymers and are able to self-reproduce and evolve on the basis of template synthesis of their polymer components" to "Life is what the scientific establishment (probably after some healthy disagreement) will accept as life."[3]

One geneticist reviewed 123 definitions to find their commonalities and decided on "self-reproduction with variations." Yet contradictions quickly challenged the definition. A biochemist pointed out, for example, that "A computer virus performs self-reproduction with variations. It is not alive."[4]

The conundrum was then tackled by a philosopher, Carol Cleland, who essentially argued that it was futile to beat our heads against the wall trying to come up with a final, naileddown definition of life. The problem, she said, is in the nature of definitions. "We don't want to know what the word *life* means to us," she said. "We want to know what *life* is."[5] Such words are abstract representations of real phenomena. Life is an actual phenomenon wherein vibrancy, animation, and energy exist in some things and not others. We see it in hummingbirds and lichen, but not in couches and fences.

This inability to fix upon a word brings us back to grace. We can work through the definitions. We can define grace as *participation or partnership with the divine.* We can call it *divine means of help or strength, given through the bounteous mercy and love of Jesus Christ,* as described in the Bible Dictionary.[6] We can find additional explanations in Webster's Dictionary or in the broader Christian or other religious faiths. We might even be able to discover something in the secular world—maybe in a concept like flow. An understanding of the historical underpinnings of the word can give us a foundation from which to build. We can refine our own definitions as a result. All these efforts are worthwhile.

My primary interest, however, is in collecting the iterations in order to understand, bodily and in my daily experience, what it is to live with grace. I don't want merely to gain an intellectual understanding. That's interesting but not transformative. What does gracing look like on a Tuesday in July?

What's it like to interact with my child while yoked with Christ, and how does the experience differ when I'm unyoked? When wrestling through sickness or pain, how does gracing transform me? Sitting on a park bench, I want to intuit that all creatures are part of holiness. Like the Trappist monk Thomas Merton observed on the intersection of Fourth and Walnut in Louisville's shopping district, I'd love to grasp that everyone is "walking around shining like the sun."[7] How does experiential knowing blow a hole through any abstract definition?

In collecting the moments of godly participation, I am interested in the times that feel holy, connected, and awake—and in letting the other ones die. Each of these iterations is a seashell. I'll reach for gracing again and again. The shells point me to my ocean. All the iterations steer me toward the bigger picture of a life lived with Jesus—the deep and universal living water, and the animating source of a life well lived.

Salvation means living this kind of life. We're saved when we are joined at the hip with God in our specializing, transforming, partnering, creating, teaching, attending, redeeming, wrestling, playing, resting, storytelling, returning, perceiving, and oneing.

The kingdom of heaven, Jesus says, is like a mustard seed, like yeast, like a treasure hidden in a field, like a merchant searching for pearls, like a net cast for fish (Matt. 13:31–48). It's for the earthy and the everyday, and not reserved for a future celestial prize or extraordinary burning bush. From my vantage point, it's like a shell on the beach. Like air. It's an experience of gracing. The kingdom of heaven is for now—for a Tuesday in July.

It's for this dusky summer evening, when the scent of dust and rain and a pinch of fireworks hangs suspended in the air. I walk with Michael. He takes my hand, but the wrong thumb is on top. We've been around long enough to know our hands fit best interlaced the other way, so we break the grip for a redo.

We walk around the cherry pits on the sidewalk, my flip-flops clapping against my feet and the still-wet pavement. We cross the road, breaking our grip again for Michael to cross over to my left, closest to the road—that polite, old-fashioned thing he does which shows his willingness to bodily shield me from potential attackers, drunken drivers, and stray baseballs.

We hold hands again. I notice the brave weeds bursting from seams between the curb and street and admire the patch of well-tended pink daylilies. The rhythm of crickets and the spray of evening sprinklers call out time like the ticking of a clock. The scent of suburban petunias, freshly mowed grass, and new asphalt mingles with easy conversation and silence. The lamppost casts a halo against the purple sky, where the moon sinks like a sigh behind the clouds.

So Jesus comes like a thief in the night (1 Thess. 5:2).

The kingdom of heaven is here.

Michael squeezes my hand.
I squeeze back.

Poems of Grace

Time and again, my family has taught me about grace.

For Christmas one year, I wrote each of my family members a poem that I rolled, tied with twine, and tucked into the Christmas tree. Each concrete image of each poem drew from specific memories. Writing drew me to each child and to my husband, which simultaneously drew me to Jesus, whose birth we were celebrating. These poems were a catalyst for this book as I thought about themes like creating, resting, and collecting.

James Joyce wrote, "In the particular is contained the universal."[1] When goodness, truth, and beauty are found in one child, cranky and disheveled as they may be, we learn of its holy presence in all God's family. And when we are cranky and disheveled, dismissing our children's rocks or crayon drawings as mundane or ordinary, we may as well be, in the words of Tish Harrison Warren, "standing before the Grand Canyon or the Sistine Chapel and rolling our eyes."[2] The whole of the ocean is in one shell.

Engaging in this embodied earthly experience with my particular group of people and in my particular corner of the world, the vastness of God is illuminated. I hope that what I've seen and learned from my people will help you see and learn from yours. And then, in our separate particulars we'll all come nearer our shared universal.

For My Julia

A thousand years ago I held you in my arms. Or was it yesterday? "Milk, baby, lambie doll," you said. We rocked. I sang you songs about Baby Beluga and My Only Sunshine. Your heavy eyes drooped, and your sucking slowed. Silent and fluid as air, I carried you to your crib. You jolted awake, then started to cry. I tried soothing you again, but you and your tears grew up and bled into the fabric of my jeans because he'd left, and your little heart was broken.

Oh, Baby Mine.

A thousand years ago you went to kindergarten. Or was it yesterday? A momentary look of panic crossed your face—but then resolve. You squared your shoulders, your pink and green backpack dwarfing your little frame. Declining my offer to walk you to class, you marched resolutely through the sea of big kids, your pigtails trailing. When I picked you up, you told me all about porcupines and perfect paragraphs. You brought home a goldfish and a prize for your Halloween poem. And you laughed that laugh of yours—the one that fills the house.

Uninhibited like chimes.

A thousand years ago you sold your dollhouse. Or was it yesterday? All the little rooms and cupboards, and the accessories for which you'd diligently saved, graced some other girl's room and made way for iPods, nail polish and accelerating time. You turned your attention to your own little room, coloring it lime green and purple. And anything sunny yellow, of course. But changing your mind, you upcycled with sophisticated neutrals, homemade pillows, and grown-up soda cups and straws.

Your signature style.

A thousand years ago you drove away. Or was it yesterday? It was our fault—mine and Dad's. We taught you how. At first, you barricaded the intersection after you turned the wheel too late, heading for the corner house with the brown rail fence and picture-perfect vegetable garden. I took the wheel to straighten us out—the growing row of cars waiting patiently. We turned the corner and suddenly it was only you, driving your little red car in Logan, smiling out your window and waving goodbye.

Courage like nails.

A thousand years ago you sang me a song. Or was it yesterday? Channeling your Judy Garland, you sang the first verse: "The wind began to switch; the house, to pitch!"—all crisply annunciated, riding on a broomstick. Not to be outdone, the next verse passionately insisted, "I am a girl like you," followed too soon by "the start of something new." . . . My baby in a big girl's dress. At last, you sang about seeing life in pink, and the words were all in French. And something about Baby Beluga too.

Wild and free.

All my Love, *Mom*

For My Caleb

A long time ago, before sand timers, sundials, and alarm clocks, God saw the chaos in the darkness, and He organized it. He wound up the sun, flipped the switch, and watched it shine—and then proclaimed that it was good.

He was a creator—just like you.

When the grasshopper clung to the concrete wall, defying gravity, you pondered him with awe. Placing hand and foot against the wall, you trusted—following his lead. Sand on the beach became cinnamon, sprinkled on the ground as food for seagulls. Sidewalks and bare bellies became the canvas for your art. And then you took the rusted pile of Dune Buggy behind the gate, set it ablaze only once, and brought it, sputtering, back to life. Always you saw mathematical awe—in patterns, in infinite time and negative space, in the simple and elegant truth of primes.

You are a creator of wonder.

Your chaos of randomly assorted Legos became games, cities, worlds, working calculators, and animations with stories all their own. Again and again, you assembled the disordered pieces of your school bus puzzle, laid the completed masterpiece next to your pillow and dreamt of your creations. You parked your Hot Wheels cars in long, straight rows, aligned the colors of your Rubik's cubes, and then rearranged—organizing and playing with the thoughts in your head.

You are a creator of order.

Once I built a Rapunzel tower with the Lincoln logs, tall and straight with a small window up top. Each time I played, I built the same tower. But you took those logs and saw wild and magical config-urations—every time a different possibility. The predictable figure-eight layout of the GeoTrax gave way to hills, caverns, and infinite crisscrossing paths. Falling marbles careened past their running companions, each on a sight-seeing tour all their own. Turning each corner, you saw a different path because you put it there.

You are a creator of possibilities.

I love to watch you play the piano; uncompelled by assignment, your body leads the music, and your fingers keep the time. In composing a song, random notes took shape, painting lovely colors. Your music, and all your other worlds, are without number—Vikings, sea creatures, and Escher-like vistas take center stage. Loveliness discovered with a dot on a page, a word in a dictionary, a number in your mind.

You are a creator of beauty.

Even after the sun went down, in your dreams, you continued to create. Once you dreamt of a cup—half full or half empty? Neither—all full because you took it and filled it up.

And I saw that it was all so good.

All my Love, *Mom*

For My Dylan

Occasionally the winter-gray sky is swept by a massive flock of birds—each bird unique, yet moving in unison as if with one brain, pulled through the sky on a twisting string. The pool of birds flows toward the sun, but mid-air changes its mind. Unapologetically, it turns headlong toward the mountains, at times undulating like fields of grass. Or else falling like a freight train.

At dawn, the flock ascends unexpectedly from behind a tree. Boom! Like fireworks it makes its grand debut. With just as much power, grace, and unpredictability, you came sweeping into my life. As if sensing your energy, I cried to the nurse that you were coming—"I've gotta push!" She came running just in time, but the doctor was too slow. . . . Always the world was too slow. Slippery and wet, you came and finished my cry.

The flock veers left, pulling stragglers up like pants but waiting for no one. Then suddenly the flock contracts, pooling all its energy for a startling shot across the sky. Like you, the flock craves wind against its face. A sliver of a boy, you raced up the block on your red balance bike—a nugget on fire.

Turning the corner, you raced down the block on your two-wheeler without training wheels. And losing no time, you launched yourself from scooters, skateboards, Ripstiks, Hoverboards, unicycles, motorbikes, and snowboards—content with nothing short of rocket fuel implanted in your bones. Anything to give you wings.

Once, one of the flock went rogue—a renegade bird breaking from the synchronous mass. A trend setter and rule breaker, following the beat of its own drum. Long past the time it was socially acceptable, you were Elmo's biggest fan. And the boy who ditched the sandwiches, opting for salads instead, inspiring starry-eyed girls to do the same. A fan of both Yo-Yo Ma's cello and Survivor's "Eye of the Tiger." A Bob Ross painting on a trampoline. Lover of both scarlet macaws and pigeons. You blazed your own way, an eclectic canvas of contradictions.

At sunset, the flock dips low to the ground, dragging its toe along the water's glassy surface. It was a flying fish or a swimming bird—you never could be sure. But now you were low enough to let me in—to let me fly a little while with you. A shared joke. An impish smile. A song you'd never sung before. You turned and let me wipe the sand from your toes. But then you popped up like a cork and disappeared into the dark. My little Tarzan on a vine.

All my Love, *Mom*

For My Jonah

Once upon a time, wrapped inside a dream, I found a large wooden wardrobe full of heavy coats—thick and musty. I walked inside because, of course, I was curious. Past thick fur, I walked in deeper, reaching out my hands in expectation of the wardrobe's wooden back. But instead, the world opened, and I found myself in a densely wooded forest, blanketed in crusted snow.

Inside the woods I found a world you'd seen a thousand times. All the things you'd come to know. Peeking in, one lighted tree stood tall—gently painted by a hovering star. Coming near, I saw you as a babe upon my lap, cozy in the rocking chair. Blue eyes fixed upon the tree; you watched the Christmas lights cast ethereal shadows on the wall. A Starry Night of stillness. In my mind, I took a picture of you—this believing soul. Lover of light, magic, and everything good.

Beside the tree there was a shelf, carefully maintained. An artist's mural of treasures, you had arranged Halloween pumpkins, plastic dinosaurs, Christmas globes, pinecones, whittled sticks, porcelain birds, acorns, and seeds that spilled their cotton in a lidded jar. Stacks of wrinkled papers held too tight by eager strokes of thickly planted paint. An archive of trophies—Lego creations, broken seashells and lumps of clay. A shrine and tribute to the truth you saw. And Jesus watching over all.

Walking behind the tree, I started up a mountain. A heroic feat for me—it was mere child's play for you. Knowing of my struggle, you took my hand. You the parent, I the child. And we reached the top together—a painted "Y" upon the mountain's face. Once there we sat to rest and catching my breath you pulled from your pocket a book. You read to me a well-worn paragraph with words as lovely as your shrine—words of whimsy and play. Delight too big to hold.

Gaining strength, we journeyed on. Around the bend we found an injured nest of birds. Too young to fly, the fledgling's chests were all that moved—clothed only in transparent peach fuzz. Those who did not live, we buried in a shallow grave—a prayer in flower petals. For the living birds, we fashioned an awkward nest cradled in a nearby tire, a home we hoped the mother bird would see. But momentarily distracted, we turned to find the birds had gone—surely flying to your treasure trove upon the shelf.

In searching for that place again, we came upon a lamppost from a long-forgotten dream. We pressed our bodies forward, trudging deep through fur—emerging, stumbling, from the wardrobe. Older now and looking back, I found a solitary acorn lying dusty on the wooden floor. A treasure from your Narnia—a shadow of your dream more tangible than rocks. Picking it up, I stored it. Deep inside my pocket. Wrapped my fist around it. Held it close.

All my Love, *Mom*

For My Michael

Sitting on a beach with you, not doing much. Mostly just breathing. Taking in that salty drink of sunshine. And I am completely happy—like, deep down in your bones, hot air balloons and strawberry shortcake kind of happy. The good strawberries—you know, those wild, sweet ones from back in the day, not the ginormously bland Costco ones.

Sometimes they say that marriage is hard—a sweaty marathon of an uphill both ways kind of struggle. That it takes this clench-jawed, Herculean sort of determination—all worth it in the end, mind you, but that the prize comes only to those who embody the self-sacrifice and superpowers of actual saints.

Funny, I never saw it that way. Sitting here with you, it's as simple as breathing.

It doesn't take much. I never needed spectacular adventure, though we've had a few punctuating moments when, in awe, we held our breath. Remember that slinking shadow of a shark, lurking in the belly of a cresting wave? Or that massive whale launch straight into the slippery sky? That time we played out in the cold December sea, just because we could? And when, like tiny drones, that school of flying fish leapt forward on a mission, whirring and slapping past our boat?

But after we stop to catch our breath, it's quiet. Past words. Simply squeeze my hand and I'll squeeze yours. A lazy afternoon on a hammock, folded together, not knowing whose limbs are whose. The crook of your arm for my head. The sun reaching down between palm leaves, like warm fingers. Hovering in that soft space between sleep and wakefulness, where either destination will do. Chests rising slow. In and out, an easy rhythm. And I am happy—like, red snapper fresh from an early-morning fisherman, Zen monk in a swimming pool of goose down feathers kind of happy.

Take me home and pass the maté. I'll pass it back. We'll cuddle on the couch and drink from the same straw, with a little bit of sugar. We'll turn on the fake Netflix fire, crackling on the TV. I'll read you poetry—breezy words about "a red wheel barrow, glazed with rain water, beside the white chickens." And we'll just breathe the same air—not the carbon dioxy kind, mind you, the kind that simply means you are there. Warm, close, and all I need.

All my Love, *Hannah*

For My Izzy

I like you,

little Doggus Woggus.

All my Love, *Mom*

When sunlight meets still water, some of its rays ricochet back, shimmering, to create a canvas of what it sees: mountain peaks, red sandstone cliffs, or rows of pine. Reflection creates a mirror—a reimagining of the original landscape.

These reflection questions are designed for a similar purpose. As your experiences, relationships, and thoughts meet mine, my hope is that you will reflect back an image, a likeness of gracing informed by your own life. In the process, I hope you also discover fragments of the God whose image bearer you are.

Chapter One: Specializing

1. When was I immersed in a specific activity or vocation that lit me up? What specific details stand out?

2. In what work do I find myself immersed in grace, participating as a unique voice in the body of Christ?

3. What divinely unique gifts do I have to offer in my relationships, work, and service?

Chapter Two: Transforming

1. How does my view of the world differ from when I was a child?

2. When were my paradigms deconstructed during a specific period of life? What held and rooted me through the disorienting process?

3. What is holding me now?

Chapter Three: Partnering

1.　What is one of my habits or routines in which my relationship with God seems absent?

2.　What is one of my frequent routines that feels like an intentional practice of seeking God?

3.　When was the last time I felt like I was living a life in Christ? What was that like?

____

____

____

____

____

____

____

____

____

____

____

____

____

____

____

____

____

Chapter Four: Creating

1. What experiences, personality traits, interests, limitations, and gifts do I have to work with in creating the canvas of my life?

2. When have I experienced grace as a cocreator with God? What did we create together, and what was that experience like?

3. What would I like to create with God in the future?

Chapter Five: Teaching

1. What analogies, stories, or teachings have been most helpful to me in understanding the true nature of grace?

2. What analogies, stories, or teachings clouded my view of grace, causing me to misunderstand its true nature?

3. What have been my "Sermons on the Lawn"— life experiences that helped me more fully recognize grace and embrace its presence?

Chapter Six: Attending

1. When have my needs been attended to by someone else within the body of Christ?

2. In the past, who have I noticed struggling to participate in the body of Christ? What did I learn that can help me attend better to others' needs in the future?

3. Whose needs can I attend to now? What might attending with grace look like with this specific person?

Chapter Seven: Redeeming

1. How have the sins, pains, weaknesses, and failures of others weighed me down?

2. What scars of mine have been redeemed or transformed into gifts of perspective, growth, compassion, or strength? How did that happen? Did I feel God in the process?

3. In what ways have I burdened others? How has grace helped them transform these burdens into gifts?

Chapter Eight: Wrestling

1. What have been the major wrestles of my life? What "collateral beauty" have I discovered through these wrestles?

2. When did I confront a totally unjust or evil situation? Was God there? If so, what was God's role?

Chapter Nine: Playing

1. When have I played recently—in a relaxed, delightful, spontaneous, agenda-free way? What was that experience like?

2. Do I ever feel guilty after relaxed and agenda-free play?

3. How can I cultivate more experiences of grace-filled play?

____

____

____

____

____

____

____

____

____

____

____

____

____

____

____

____

Chapter Ten: Resting

1. What rituals or practices bring a restful aura into my day? How does my day improve when I make intentional time for these?

2. When do I feel most scattered or frantic? What habits or routines might be contributing to a lack of rest?

3. What were my best Sabbaths? What made those Sabbaths restful or holy?

Chapter Eleven: Storytelling

1. When did I see the light or goodness in someone I thought was different, wrong, or outside the proper mold?

2. How was I changed by this experience?

3. How does the story that I am a child of God, with a spark of divinity, impact me? How does it either complement or contrast with the other stories I tell myself?

Chapter Twelve: Returning

1. How does it feel to re-enter the flow of grace after being away?

2. When have I felt my heart soften towards someone? What was that like?

3. What is one of my relationships that feels stuck? How is grace inviting me to return to my true self, to this person, or to God?

Chapter Thirteen: Perceiving

1. In what ways is my perception constrained? What facets of
    my biology, culture, religion, or nationality limit my view of
    the whole?

2. When did I interact with someone who saw a different
    piece of the whole than I did? How did that expand my
    own awareness?

3. How can I expand my umwelt? What relationships, books, or
    ideas would I like to engage with so I can participate more
    fully as a moved mover?

Chapter Fourteen: Oneing

1. When have I learned about myself through individuation—separating myself from other people? What strengths and weaknesses have come to light through that process?

2. What have I learned about myself through interdependence and one-ness with others? What strengths and weaknesses have I observed?

3. How would I approach my life differently if I believed mortality to be a group project?

Thank you to my talented editor, Jana Riess, whose critical eye and perceptive feedback improved my writing from start to finish. She guided me in improving my delivery, message, and flow, while also being a generous and encouraging voice. Her mentorship was invaluable.

Thank you to my friend J. Kirk Richards for providing the exquisite artwork for this book. I have loved Kirk's work for years, and his artwork gives beautiful form to what I have hoped to express through words. I am grateful his art serves as such a moving companion to this book.

Thank you to Faith Matters for supporting an unaffiliated, first-time author. I have loved the writing, conversations, and events they have curated through recent years, and I am profoundly honored to work with them. Their vision of an expansive gospel, drawing from truth and beauty wherever it is found, is one that resonates deeply with me. To David and Kristin Turnbull, thank you for the initial vote of confidence, and to Bill Turnbull and Zachary Davis and the rest of the team at Faith Matters, thank you for seeing it through.

Thank you to my mom, Sandy Packard, who once told me, "I hope you write a book someday," and whose careful attention to detail improved my work. Thank you to my dad, Dennis Packard, who explored ideas with me and helped me think critically and spaciously. Thank you to my other mother, Marjorie Crowther, whose tender responses to my writing gave me hope, and to my niece, Halee Crowther, who reminded me to ignore the mean girls in my head.

Thank you to those who spent time with my writing. Thank you to Amy Egbert, Lisa Harper, Miriam Wood, Alicia Blair, Markell Horner, Raylyn Poulson, Bree Gracesun, Anna Dunn, Alisia Sansom, Seth Packard, Angela Norden, Debra Packard, Tom Christofferson, and Steven Peck for their feedback and encouragement. And to my very informal writing group, thank you for giving me a gentle place to practice forming words from nebulous feelings and incomplete ideas. Writing is undoubtedly better with friends.

Thank you to the many insightful writers who have informed my thoughts, many of whom I have quoted and referenced throughout this book. I feel as if they have graciously mentored me through paradigm-shifting, expansive ways of seeing. The resulting understanding has revealed the gospel to me as bona fide good news. In particular, Adam Miller's writing was pivotal in teaching me about grace; his writing has breathed new life into old ideas for me.

Thank you to my children—Julia, Caleb, Dylan, and Jonah. You are my heart's joy and the original inspiration for this book. In learning from you and loving you, grace has moved from the abstract to the real. I stand in awe of your gifts and unique contributions to the world, and I am profoundly grateful to be your mom.

And finally, thank you to my husband and devoted friend, Michael. Thank you for our beautiful partnership. By knowing me better than anyone and still loving me better than anyone, you help me understand how God must see all of us. Thank you for your feedback on my many drafts, for being willing to invest our resources in this project, and for believing in what I had to offer. Te amo, mi amor.

ENDNOTES

AN INTRODUCTION

1. Adam Miller, *Grace Is Not God's Back-Up Plan: An Urgent Paraphrase of Paul's Letter to the Romans* (McKinney, TX: CreateSpace Independent Publishing Platform, 2015); Ashley Mae Hoiland, *One Hundred Birds Taught Me to Fly: The Art of Seeking God* (Provo, UT: Brigham Young University Neal A. Maxwell Institute, 2016).

1

1. Marilynne Robinson, *Gilead* (New York: Farrar, Straus and Giroux, 2004), 245.

2. Annie Dillard, *Pilgrim at Tinker Creek* (New York: Harper Perennial Modern Classics, 2013), 10.

3. Dillard, *Pilgrim at Tinker Creek,* 36.

4. C.S. Lewis, *The Great Divorce* (Toronto, Ontario: Macmillan, 1969), 6.

5. C.S. Lewis, *The Great Divorce,* 6.

6. Tish Harrison Warren, *Liturgy of the Ordinary: Sacred Practices in Everyday Life* (Downers Grove, IL: IVP Books, 2016), 94.

7. Hugh Hudson, *Chariots of Fire* (London, England: Enigma Productions, 1981).

8. Hudson, *Chariots of Fire.*

9. Robin Wall Kimmerer, *Braiding Sweetgrass: Indigenous Wisdom, Scientific Knowledge, and the Teachings of Plants* (Minneapolis, MN: Milkweed Editions, 2013), 297.

10. Matthew Brown, *The Man Who Knew Infinity* (Hollywood, CA: Paramount Home Entertainment, 2016).

11. Robert Ellsberg, *By Little and By Little: The Selected Writings of Dorothy Day* (New York: Alfred A. Knopf, 1983), 187.

2

1. "We Lived with God," The Church of Jesus Christ of Latter-Day Saints, accessed March 16, 2024, https://www.churchofjesuschrist.org/media/video/2011-06-03-we-lived-with-god.

3

1. Adam Miller, *An Early Resurrection: Life in Christ Before You Die* (Salt Lake City, UT: Deseret Book, 2018), 11–13.

2. Tish Harrison Warren, *Liturgy of the Ordinary: Sacred Practices in Everyday Life* (Downers Grove, IL: IVP Books, 2016).

4

1. Thomas Keating, "Out of a Stone," in *The Secret Embrace* (Temple Rock Company, 2018).

2. Dieter F. Uchtdorf, "Happiness, Your Heritage," *Ensign,* November 2008, 119.

3. Dorothy Sayers, *The Mind of the Maker* (San Francisco, CA: HarperCollins, 1979), 192.

4. Chris Guillebeau, *The Art of Non-Conformity: Set Your Own Rules, Live the Life You Want, and Change the World* (New York: TarcherPerigee, 2010).

5. Terryl and Fiona Givens, *The God Who Weeps: How Mormonism Makes Sense of Life* (Salt Lake City, UT: Deseret Book, 2017), 50.

5

1. Richard Rohr, "The Task Within the Task," Center for Action and Contemplation, January 29, 2023, https://cac.org/daily-meditations/the-task-within-the-task-2023-01-29/.

2. Bob Clark, *A Christmas Story* (Metro-Goldwyn-Mayer, 1983).

3. Stephen E. Robinson, "Believing Christ: A Practical Approach to the Atonement," BYU Speeches, May 29, 1990, https://speeches.byu.edu/talks/stephen-e-robinson/believing-christ-practical-approach-atonement/.

4. Adam S. Miller, *Grace Is Not God's Backup Plan: An Urgent Paraphrase of Paul's Letter to the Romans* (McKinney, TX: CreateSpace Independent Publishing Platform, 2015).

5. Brad Wilcox, "His Grace is Sufficient," BYU Speeches, July 12, 2011, https://speeches.byu.edu/talks/brad-wilcox/his-grace-is-sufficient/.

6. Samuel M. Brown, *First Principles and Ordinances* (Provo, UT: Neal A. Maxwell Institute for Religious Scholarship, 2014), 48–49.

6

1. Robert M. Daines, "Sir, We Would Like to See Jesus," *Liahona*, November 2023, 14–15.

2. Virginia Hatch and Richard O. Cowan, *The Colonia Juárez Temple: A Prophet's Inspiration* (Provo, UT: Religious Studies Center, Brigham Young University, 2009), 20.

3. Orson F. Whitney, in *Ninety-Eighth Annual Conference of the Church of Jesus Christ of Latter-day Saints* (Salt Lake City, UT: The Church of Jesus Christ of Latter-day Saints, 1928), 59.

4. Oliver Wendell Holmes to Lady Pollock, October 24, 1902, in *Holmes-Pollock Letters: The Correspondence of Mr Justice Holmes and Sir Frederick Pollock, 1874–1932*, ed. Mark DeWolfe Howe, 2nd ed. (Cambridge, MA: Belknap Press of Harvard University Press, 1961), 109.

5. Richard Rohr, "Jesus' Alternative Reality," Center for Action and Contemplation, January 18, 2018, https://cac.org/daily-meditations/jesus-alternative-reality-2018-01-18/.

6. B. H. Roberts, "Book of Mormon Translation," *Improvement Era*, July 1906, 713.

7. Thomas Wirthlin McConkie, *Navigating Mormon Faith Crisis: A Simple Developmental Map* (Salt Lake City, UT: Thomas Wirthlin McConkie, 2015), 149–50.

7

1. Gregory Boyle, *Tattoos on the Heart: The Power of Boundless Compassion* (New York: Free Press, 2010), 66.

2. Fiona Givens and Terryl Givens, *The Christ Who Heals: How God Restored the Truth That Saves Us* (Salt Lake City, UT: Deseret Book, 2017), 64.

3. Sandra Bradford Packard, *The Salvation of Animals* (self-published, 2017), preface.

8

1. David B. Williams, "Tarantula Hawk," DesertUSA, accessed March 20, 2024, https://www.desertusa.com/insects/tarantula-hawks.html.

2. "The Death of Anne Elizabeth Darwin," Darwin Correspondence Project, University of Cambridge, accessed March 20, 2024, https://www.darwinproject. ac.uk/people/about-darwin/family-life/death-anne-elizabeth-darwin.

3. Robert Shuman, *The Psychology of Chronic Illness: The Healing Work of Patients, Therapists, & Families* (New York: Basic Books, 1996), 37.

4. Horatio Gates Spafford, "It Is Well," Hymnal.net, accessed March 20, 2024, https://www.hymnal.net/en/hymn/h/341.

5. Dallan Forgaill, "Be Thou My Vision, O Lord of My Heart," Hymnal.net, accessed March 20, 2024, https://www.hymnal.net/en/hymn/ns/345.

6. Joseph Smith, Letter to William W. Phelps, 27 November 1832, The Joseph Smith Papers, accessed March 20, 2024, https://www.josephsmithpapers.org/paper-summary/letter-to-william-w-phelps-27-november-1832/4.

7. Annie Dillard, *The Writing Life* (New York: Harper & Row, 1989), 74–75.

8. Francine Bennion, "A Latter-day Saint Theology of Suffering," sermon given at the Brigham Young University Women's Conference, March 28, 1986, in *At the Pulpit: 185 Years of Discourses by Latter-day Saint Women*, ed. Jennifer Reeder and Kate Holbrook (Salt Lake City, UT: Church Historian's Press, 2017), 215.

9. Bennion, "Latter-day Saint Theology of Suffering," 230.

10. Shuman, *Psychology of Chronic Illness*, 170.

9

1. Carl Sagan, *Pale Blue Dot: A Vision of the Human Future in Space* (New York: Random House, 1994), 52.

2. Ron Clements and John Musker, *Aladdin* (Burbank, CA: Walt Disney Animation Studios, 1992).

3. Lauren Swayne Barthold, "Hans-Georg Gadamer (1900–2002)," Internet Encyclopedia of Philosophy, accessed March 20, 2024, http://iep.utm.edu/gadamer/.

4. Betsy Johnson-Miller, "A Theology of Play: An Interview with Resident Scholar Brendan McInerny," Bearings Online, Collegeville Institute, February 9, 2017, https://collegevilleinstitute.org/bearings/a-theology-of-play/.

5. Johnson-Miller, "Theology of Play."

6. Lewis Thomas, *The Medusa and the Snail: More Notes of a Biology Watcher* (New York: Penguin Books, 1974), 28.

7. Daniel Quinn, *Ishmael: An Adventure of the Mind and Spirit* (New York: Bantam/Turner, 1992), 55–56.

8. Anne Lamott, quoted in Brené Brown, *The Gifts of Imperfection: Let Go of Who You Think You're Supposed to Be and Embrace Who You Are* (Center City, MN: Hazelden, 2010), 118.

9. Gerard Manley Hopkins, "As Kingfishers Catch Fire," in *Gerard Manley Hopkins: Poems and Prose* (New York: Penguin Classics, 1985), available online at Poetry Foundation, accessed March 21, 2024, https://www.poetryfoundation.org/poems/44389/as-kingfishers-catch-fire.

10. George MacDonald, quoted in C. S. Lewis, *Mere Christianity* (London: HarperCollins, 1952), 205.

10

1. Matthew Walker, *Why We Sleep: Unlocking the Power of Sleep and Dreams* (New York: Scribner, 2017).

2. Annie Dillard, *Pilgrim at Tinker Creek* (New York: Harper Perennial, 1999), 82.

3. Thomas Keating, *Open Mind, Open Heart,* 20th anniversary ed. (New York: Bloomsbury Continuum, 1986), 34.

4. "Desmond Tutu, Insisting We Are 'Made for Goodness,'" NPR, March 10, 2010, https://radio.kttz.org/2010-03-10/desmond-tutu-insisting-we-are-made-for-goodness.

5. June Eding, *How to Hug a Porcupine: Easy Ways to Hug the Difficult People in Your Life* (New York: Hatherleigh Press, 2009).

6. Abraham Joshua Heschel, *The Sabbath: Its Meaning for Modern Man* (New York: Farrar, Straus and Giroux, 1951), 14.

7. Heschel, *Sabbath,* 74.

8. Susannah Heschel, "Introduction," in Heschel, *Sabbath,* 2005 ed., vii–xvi.

9. Heschel, *Sabbath,* 21.

11

1. William Wordsworth, "Ode on Intimations of Immortality from Recollections of Early Childhood," available online at Poets.org, accessed March 21, 2024, https://poets.org/poem/ode-intimations-immortality-recollections-early-childhood.

2. Adam Miller, *Original Grace: An Experiment in Restoration Thinking* (Salt Lake City, UT: Deseret Book, 2022), 97.

3. Gregory Boyle, *Tattoos on the Heart: The Power of Boundless Compassion* (New York: Free Press, 2010), 24, 52.

4. Boyle, *Tattoos on the Heart,* 108.

12

1. Kathryn Schulz, "On Being Wrong," TED: Ideas Worth Spreading, March 2011, https://www.ted.com/talks/kathryn_schulz_on_being_wrong.

2. C. Terry Warner, *Bonds That Make Us Free: Healing Our Relationships, Coming to Ourselves* (Salt Lake City, UT: Shadow Mountain, 2001), 23–27.

3. Martin Luther King Jr., "Letter from Birmingham Jail," August 1963, available online at https://www.csuchico.edu/iege/_assets/documents/susi-letter-from-birmingham-jail.pdf.

13

1. Terry Gillam and Terry Jones, *Monty Python and the Holy Grail* (Columbia TriStar Home Video, 1975).

2. Edward O. Wilson, *Naturalist* (Washington, DC: Island Press, 1994), 295–96.

3. Ed Yong, *An Immense World: How Animal Senses Reveal the Hidden Realms around Us* (New York City: Random House, 2022).

4. Barbara Brown Taylor, *The Luminous Web: Essays on Science and Religion* (Lanham, MD: Cowley Publications, 2000), 73–74, as quoted in Brian D. McLaren, *Do I Stay Christian?: A Guide for the Doubters, the Disappointed, and the Disillusioned* (New York: St. Martin's Essentials, 2022), 173.

5. Abraham J. Heschel, *Between God and Man: An Interpretation of Judaism* (New York: Free Press Paperbacks, 1999), 25, 97–98, 119, 140–141.

6. Taylor, in McLaren, *Do I Stay Christian?*, 173.

7. Heschel, *Between God and Man,* 162.

8. Jason Olson and James Goldberg, *The Burning Book: A Jewish-Mormon Memoir* (Newburgh, IN: BCC Press, 2022), x.

9. Robin Wall Kimmerer, *Braiding Sweetgrass: Indigenous Wisdom, Scientific Knowledge, and the Teachings of Plants* (Minneapolis: Milkweed Editions, 2013), 383.

10. A. J. Arberry, *Mystical Poems of Rumi* (Chicago: University of Chicago Press, 1968), 219.

11. Alicia Lee, "Martin Luther King Jr. Explains the Meaning of Love in a Rare Handwritten Note," CNN, February 9, 2020, https://www.cnn.com/2020/02/09/us/martin-luther-king-jr-handwritten-note-for-sale-trnd/index.html.

14

1. M. Catherine Thomas, *Light in the Wilderness: Explorations in the Spiritual Life* (Salt Lake City, UT: Digital Legends Press, 2010), 203.

2. "Oneing," Center for Action and Contemplation, May 12, 2020, cac.org/daily-meditations/oneing-2020-05-12/.

3. Vanessa Guerin, ed., *Oneing: The Universal Christ* (Albuquerque, NM: CAC Publishing, 2019), 59.

4. Noah Strycker, *The Thing with Feathers: The Surprising Lives of Birds and What They Reveal about Being Human* (New York: Riverhead Books, 2014).

5. Jacob T. Baker, "'Friendship Is Like Welding Iron to Iron': The Sealing Power, the Welding Link, and the Grand Fundamental Principle of Mormonism," 4, 25–26, paper for Claremont Graduate University class taught by Richard L. Bushman, Academia.edu, Fall 2009, https://www.academia.edu/289358?Friendship_is_Like_Welding_Iron_to_Iron_The_Sealing_Power_the_Welding_Link_and_the_Grand_Fundamental_Principle_of_Mormonism.

6. Baker, "'Friendship Is Like Welding Iron to Iron,'" 25.

7. Baker, "'Friendship Is Like Welding Iron to Iron,'" 26.

8. Jeff Ashby personal interview, as quoted in Adam Grant, *Think Again: The Power of Knowing What You Don't Know* (New York: Viking, 2021), 129.

9. Richard Rohr, *The Universal Christ: How a Forgotten Reality Can Change Everything We See, Hope For, and Believe* (New York: Convergent, 2021), 16.

10. Maria Popova, "The Universe as an Infinite Storm of Beauty: John Muir on the Transcendent Interconnectedness of Nature," The Marginalian, accessed March 23, 2024, https://www.themarginalian.org/2018/05/10/john-muir-nature-writings/.

A CONCLUSION

1. Vanessa Guerin, ed., *Oneing: The Universal Christ* (Albuquerque, NM: CAC Publishing, 2019), 40.

2. T. S. Eliot, "Tradition and the Individual Talent," from *The Sacred Wood* (London: Methuen and Co., 1920), available online at Bartleby, accessed March 23, 2024, https://www.bartleby.com/200/ sw4.html.

3. Carl Zimmer, *Life's Edge: The Search for What It Means to Be Alive* (New York: Dutton, 2021), 271.

4. Zimmer, *Life's Edge*, 273.

5. Zimmer, *Life's Edge*, 279–80.

6. Bible Dictionary, "Grace," The Church of Jesus Christ of Latter-day Saints.

7. Guerin, *Oneing*, 54–55.

EPILOGUE

1. Richard Ellmann, *James Joyce* (New York: Oxford University Press, 1983), 505.

2. Tish Harrison Warren, *Liturgy of the Ordinary: Sacred Practices in Everyday Life* (Downers Grove, IL: IVP Books, 2016), 45.

COLOPHON

The text of the book is typeset in William, a modern interpretation of William Caslon's historic typeface, crafted by Maria Doreuli to honor tradition while meeting the demands of contemporary design. Chapter subheads and the reflection questions are typset in GT America, designed by Noël Leu, with Seb McLauchlan.

Printed on 60 lb Accent Opaque Text, Sustainable Forestry Initiative (SFI) Certified.

Printed by North Star Printing
in Spanish Fork, Utah

Artwork by J. Kirk Richards

Book design & typography by Cole Melanson

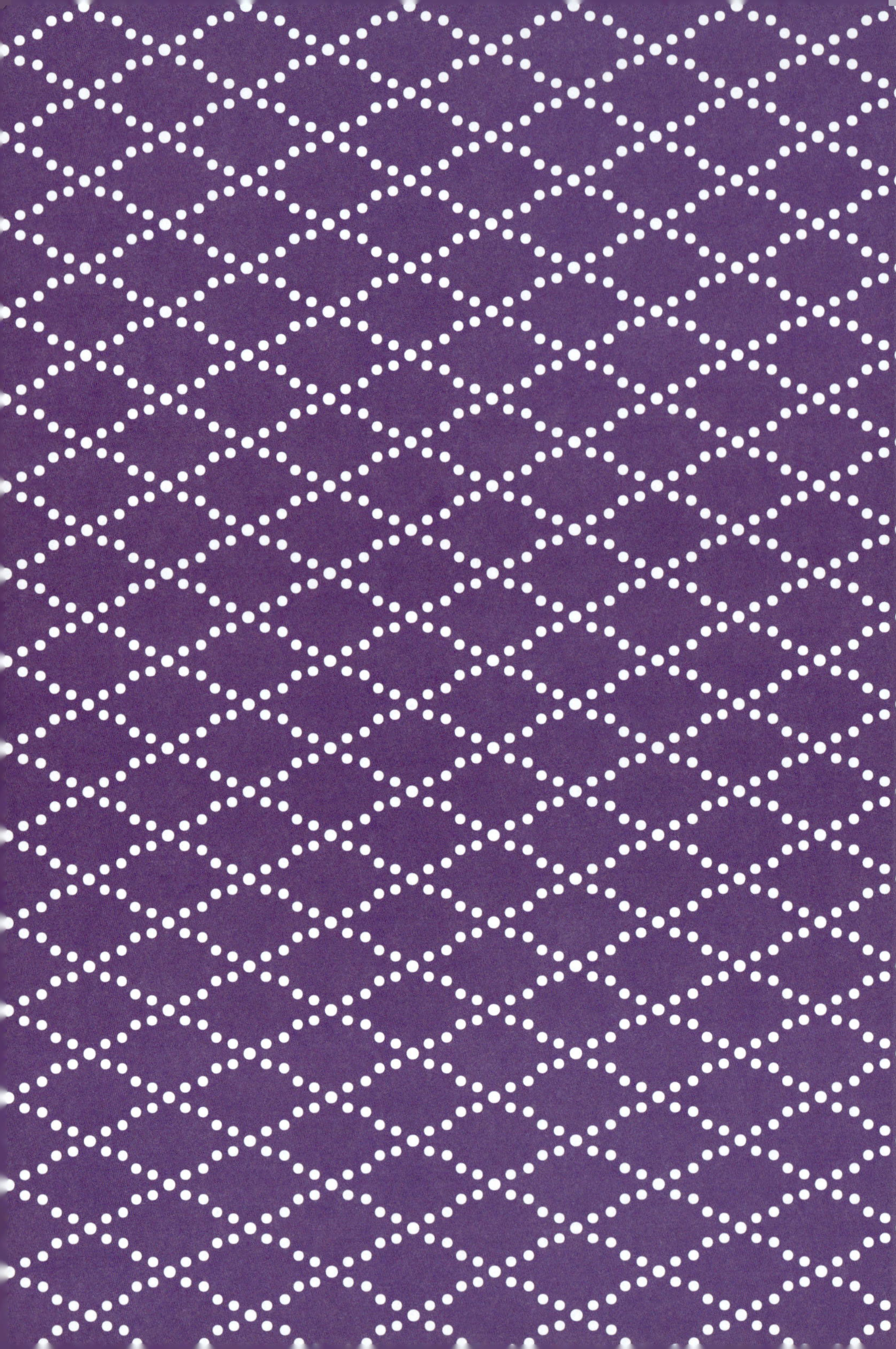